Dedication

To Ruth,
my wife of fifty-one years —
God's love gift.

Contents

From the Turnip Fields to the World

*S*mith Wigglesworth was born in 1859 in Menston, a small Yorkshire village in England, to John and Martha Wigglesworth, one of three sons and a daughter — a very poor family. Today, one hundred and forty years after his birth, he is perhaps more well-known than he was in his lifetime. And, since his death thirty-two years ago, his sermons and the books written about him have touched probably more people than he did during his life.

He began work at six years of age, pulling and cleaning turnips in the fields of a neighboring farmer. That was hard work, especially for a small boy, but even that was used by God. He learned discipline and developed an attitude toward work — and toward doing well what was entrusted to him — that stood him in good stead later in the work which God gave him to do.

From the turnip fields of Yorkshire to the mission fields of the world, Smith Wigglesworth always was a dependable and hard worker, who knew the meaning of responsibility and accountability for the tasks set before him.

This book is not intended to be a biography, nor a chronological account. As one who knew him in the years of the fullness of his ministry, I have here set down my remembrances of him with the earnest hope that the ministry the Lord entrusted to him will challenge others to discover and fulfill their own ministries.

I have been more concerned with the spiritual significance of the characteristics he displayed than with the "story of his life." He is one of the few people I have known whom I believe truly to be *conformed to the image of Christ.*

Wigglesworth's parents were not saved, but his grandmother was. She took him to a Wesleyan Methodist Mission Hall when he was eight years old. Although he was so young, he said later that he had a hunger for God; and, in fact, he could not remember a time when he did not have such a hunger.

He knew even at eight that he was not saved. He listened intently to the preaching that evening and joined sincerely in the singing. They came then to a point in the service when those dear Wesleyan brothers and sisters began to dance around the old-fashioned coal stove as they sang a song about the Lamb of God and the precious blood of the cross.

Little boy Wigglesworth danced with them and later movingly described what happened.

"Suddenly I saw that Jesus had died for *me*. Suddenly I realized that He had borne *my* sins. I lifted my heart to him, and I knew that I was born again."

Then he could sing with as much abandon as any Wesleyan Methodist! There, in that little mission hall, he got a revelation of the simplicity of conversion. For the rest of his life, he used the words of his revelation, *only believe,* over and over in his witnessing and in his messages.

Chapter 1:

I Meet "the Man Who Walked With God"

When Smith Wigglesworth stayed in our home once, he came down early one morning and told me, "God spoke to me on your bed."

"What did he say?" I asked.

"He said, 'Wigglesworth, I am going to burn you all up, until there is no more Wigglesworth, only Jesus.'"

Standing at the foot of our stairs, he raised his hands to heaven, and with tears running down his cheeks, he cried, "O, God, come and do it! I don't want them to see *me* anymore — only Jesus!"

If I had to sum up the man Smith Wigglesworth as I knew him, that one statement would be it. He lived so that people would only see Jesus.

I first met Smith Wigglesworth in 1941 as he traveled from Bradford, England, to London en route to meetings in my church, Elim Pentecostal Church, Leigh-on-Sea, Essex. We were meeting in a hired building on the north shore of the River Thames estuary, about forty miles east of London, because our church had been destroyed by a German landmine.

I met him at one London railway terminus and escorted him across the city to another where we had an appointment with a man whose wife was dying of abdominal cancer. This man was seeking the Lord's help through Wigglesworth. Our train to Leigh-on-Sea was due to leave in a few minutes, so the man accompanied us for part of the journey.

As soon as the train started, Wigglesworth said out loud, "Jesus is up. Jesus is down. Jesus is up."

I was puzzled, and so was the man.

This man of God — who was so much an "original," so much an individual, that to some he seemed eccentric — continued:

"It says in John 3:13, 'No man hath ascended up to heaven, but he that came down from heaven, even the Son of man which is in heaven.'

"You see, my brother," he said, "Jesus is in heaven with all power. I reach out the hand of faith and touch him. His power flows down through me. I stretch out the hand of compassion and faith and touch the sick and the needy. They are healed and begin to praise the Lord. The life of Jesus goes back to Him in worship. My brothers, that is the cycle of life in the Holy Spirit."

Then Wigglesworth turned to me saying, "Come on, Brother Stormont, let us pour life into this fellow."

Without regard for the other people in the railway carriage with us, he stood up — and I with him — and prayed in a firm voice, "Lord, pour Your life into this man."

Turning to the man, he said, "Go home and lay your hands on your wife's stomach, and she will be healed."

Months later, I met the man's pastor, who told me the woman's healing happened just as Wigglesworth had said it would.

Wigglesworth would have been distressed at the many books that have been written about him, but he would have redeemed the situation by saying with Paul, "Be ye followers of me, even as I also am of Christ" (1 Cor. 11:1).

He did not want people to copy him but many tried. He was totally himself, and he wanted other people to be themselves. Sometimes it was very amusing to see those who copied him. Some students at a San Francisco Bible institute noticed that when Wigglesworth was preaching, he would stroke his mustache. After he left, many of the students when preaching could be seen stroking "the substance of things hoped for, the evidence of things not seen!"

What God's Word said of Moses is, in its own measure, true of Smith Wigglesworth: "There arose not a prophet since in Israel like unto Moses, whom the Lord knew face to face" (Deut. 34:10).

That should have a challenge in it for every Christian. We cannot be Moses or Wigglesworth, yet we can press on to know God face to face.

While in our home and at my request, Wigglesworth usually led us in prayer before meals. He would start off most of the time by singing a chorus, then in confident belief, he would thank God for the food.

One day after the main course, as my wife served an apple pie, she apologized by saying, "I'm sorry, Brother Wigglesworth, this pie isn't up to standard."

Both my wife and I were taken aback by his response.

"Shut up, woman! No complaints. The blessing is on it! Once we have prayed over our food, it is sanctified, and we must never complain or apologize!"

He took the Word of God seriously: "For every creature of God is good and nothing to be refused, if it be received with thanksgiving: for it is sanctified by the word of God and prayer" (1 Tim. 4:4,5).

Because of his unique personality, even his close friends tended to look at him with astonishment at times. At another meal with us, something occurred of which I soon became ashamed, but it reveals his attitude of walking in love so well that I will tell it.

He had made one of his extraordinary remarks, and I glanced at my wife and winked.

He caught sight of my wink and simply said, "Brother, Proverbs 10, verse 10."

I had no need to read it, because I knew the verse said: "He that winketh with the eye causeth sorrow."

Blushingly, I apologized, but I had learned my lesson!

Another proverb came to my mind: "Faithful are the wounds of a friend" (Prov. 27:6).

At the end of a series of meetings he had with us, he told the congregation he would pray for each one as each left the building.

He said, "Brother Stormont and I will stand by one of the exits, and you must all go out by that door."

He had chairs placed on each side of the aisle and stood on one while I stood on the other. We laid hands on each of a happy, seeking, and believing congregation. One man among those people stood out to me at the time.

Later, he told me, "As hands were laid on me, I was filled with the power of God. My life was changed."

Indeed it was. He went on into full-time service for God and served Him effectively until his homecall. The man, Cyril Lyndon, became a close friend of ours.

Another evening, my wife drove Wigglesworth to a meeting in another church, and on the way home, the car broke down. He was unperturbed. He just talked to "Father," and very soon help appeared in the form of a man who had been at the meeting. The man arranged for the car to be taken care of then brought Wigglesworth and my wife home.

Wigglesworth told us, "He is a very kind man, but there is something wrong with his life that must be put right if he is to have any blessing from God."

We knew his discernment was right, because we knew the man and his life. At the time, Wigglesworth was eighty years of age. An old man, tired after ministering the Word and praying for many people, still he was sensitive to God. He lived so close to God at all times that he perceived people's needs, and at the same time, he was part of "the cycle of life in the Holy Spirit" so that he could minister to those needs as people were ready to receive.

Chapter 2:

Rough Kindness

*M*any times I am asked, "Did Wigglesworth really hit people when he prayed for them?"

My answer is, "Yes, sometimes."

He also was very blunt in his speech at times. Once a man said to him, "You believe in divine healing. What are you doing wearing glasses?"

Sensing insincerity, Wigglesworth said, "And what are you doing with that bald head?"

He felt bluntness and roughness were necessary. He said you have to get people's attention before you can do anything for them. He certainly got their attention! Secondly, he knew when he was dealing with sin and sickness that he was in direct conflict with the devil. The vigor of his attack on the devil came out in his methods. One day I asked him why he hit people.

He said with a smile, "I don't hit them — I hit the devil!"

When I said I did not know you could hit the devil with your fist, he replied, "You're learning."

Here are some examples of his "rough kindness."

• A Salvation Army lassie came forward for prayer wearing her regulation straw bonnet. She was crippled and walked with a cane. As he prayed for her, he shook her so vigorously that her bonnet fell off. She was totally unmindful of the fact for, as she was ministered to, the power of God seemed to shoot through every part of her body.

She dropped her cane saying, "I shall not need that any more," and moving around the building, she demonstrated that she was completely healed.

• A farmer in Kent went up for prayer for a stomach problem. Wigglesworth said, "Stand there"; then he hit the man amidships saying, "In the name of Jesus, be healed!" The man was healed instantly.

• Justus du Plessis, brother of the late David du Plessis who became known as "Mr. Pentecost," interpreted for Smith Wigglesworth during his meetings throughout South Africa. Du Plessis was for many years general secretary of the Apostolic Faith Church of South Africa. He told of how in one meeting, a big Afrikaans woman came for prayer, and Wigglesworth hit her as he prayed.

She said, "Oh, that's the way, is it?" and hit him back! But the next night she was back and asked for an opportunity to make a public apology for hitting the servant of the Lord. After she got home the night before, she had discovered that every trace of her illness was gone.

John Carter, former general secretary of the Assemblies of God of Great Britain and Ireland, once related to me an amazing account:

> I was in Australia, one of two speakers at a Bible conference. The other speaker was the principal of the Commonwealth Bible College of Australia. This man said to me, "My father was a Methodist preacher. He developed cancer of the throat and wore bandages around his throat at all times to hide and protect painful cancerous sores. He believed in a general way in prayer for healing, but hearing of Wigglesworth and (some of the claims made for his ministry), he decided to check him out.

There was a meeting at Melbourne, and he went to see for himself. As he listened, he was convinced and went forward for prayer at the end of the service. Smith Wigglesworth asked him what was wrong, then slapped my father's neck hard. The astonishing thing was that my father could hardly stand even the bandages around his throat because his neck was so painful, but when Wigglesworth slapped him, he felt no pain at all. In fact, he didn't even notice the slap!

Then Wigglesworth said to him, "Go home. Take those bandages off in the morning, and you will find the growths have gone." He returned home, went to bed and slept, when previously severe pain had kept him awake for hours. The next morning, my father removed the bandages, and the growths had disappeared entirely. There was not even a scar or mark left.

Wigglesworth was not averse to using the same principle of rough kindness on himself that he did on others. I worked for eighteen months with John Nelson Parr at Bethshan Tabernacle, Manchester, who had Wigglesworth for services. He told me that one day the evangelist was in pain from a bad back and asked Parr to pray for him. Parr did, gently laying his hands on the afflicted part of the back.

"That's no good, John," said Wigglesworth. "You must 'thump' it out. Come on, pray properly!"

Parr did as he was instructed and prayed again, this time hitting Wigglesworth really hard where the pain was.

Wigglesworth shouted, "Hallelujah! That's it. It's gone!" He had taken his own medicine.

Often, he would refer to Matthew 11:12:

The kingdom of heaven suffereth violence, and the violent take it by force.

Adam Clarke described this principle as "the required violent earnestness," and Smith Wigglesworth certainly had that!

Chapter 3:

Natural Forthrightness Becomes Holy Boldness

Wigglesworth was born in Yorkshire, England, a few miles from the city of Bradford. Yorkshire people are noted for their plain speaking, and Wigglesworth was a true Yorkshireman! More importantly, his vital faith in God added power to his natural forthrightness, a boldness that can properly be called "holy boldness." He so feared God that he feared no man. He had the fearlessness that God commanded Jeremiah to have (Jer. 1:8) and an "Ezekiel forehead." (Ezek. 3:8,9.)

Some people interpreted his boldness as arrogance. However, the truth is that behind a bold demeanor was a deep sense of humility that made him totally dependent on God. He carried a deep sense of his own inability apart from God.

When he was chairman of the great Easter Convention at Preston, Lancashire, he would make short comments between the other speakers on the agenda. There was a fullness of the Spirit as he spoke, and once a man in the balcony became so excited that he burst out loudly in other tongues.

Wigglesworth looked up to where the man was and clearly called out, "You there! Be quiet. When I'm talking, it is not the time for you to speak in tongues. I like speaking in tongues more than any of you, but when someone else is talking, you are out of order to interrupt."

He believed in the liberty of the Spirit, at the same time insisting that things be done "decently and in order."

At that same convention, he was leading an afternoon meeting with hundreds present. Quite suddenly, he stopped his talk and then spoke these words: "God has shown me there are people in this meeting bound with a demon of impurity. Whoever you are, and wherever you are, stand to your feet."

I could hardly believe he would issue such a challenge openly. He did not even ask us to bow our heads. I sat on the platform weeping as I saw people rise to their feet all over the building — young men and women, middle-aged men and women, even white-haired older people. Pointing to each one, he prayed for them one by one. A young man beneath the balcony, as he was prayed for, flung his arms in the air and shouted, "I'm free! I'm free! Praise God, I'm free!"

Physically, Wigglesworth was exceptionally strong with a stocky build, although he was of medium height. The Lord used his physical strength along with the holy boldness instilled in him to deal with a witchcraft situation one night.

Wigglesworth was conducting a meeting in a long and narrow meeting room. The main entrance was in the middle of a side wall. The people were seated on movable benches. He related this incident to me personally, saying that, as he began to preach, he found himself bound in the spirit.

He said, "I shouted, but nothing happened. I took off my jacket, but nothing happened. I asked Father what was wrong, and He showed me a line of people on a bench opposite the door. They were holding hands, and I knew at once that they were spiritualists who had come to bind up the meeting.

"So I kept on preaching, but I walked off the platform and down the aisle, still preaching. When I got opposite them, I turned, took hold of the end of the bench, lifted it up, and said, 'Out, you devils!' They slid in a heap by the door, got up, and slunk out. They had not come for deliverance, so I didn't cast the devils out of them. I cast *them* out with the devils in them. We had no more problems that night."

Arne Dahl, a Norwegian preacher in America, told me of Wigglesworth's meetings in Norway. At one of them, a preacher who could not speak above a whisper came up for prayer.

After hearing the man's problem, Wigglesworth said, "Look here, man, if you were in business, doing all you could to destroy that business, yet asked me to pray for God to prosper your business, I wouldn't do it. I would tell you to sort out your methods and get your business on a proper foundation, *then* I would pray.

"Now, what is the good of me praying that God will heal your voice when you are going to destroy it again by using it wrongly? If you will learn to use your voice properly, I will pray for you."

The preacher agreed. Wigglesworth prayed, the man was healed and went on to learn that he could use his voice without abusing it, Dahl said.

The testimony of Dr. Mildred Serjeant of Lakenheath, Suffolk, England, brings out another aspect of Wigglesworth's holy boldness. Here is the account in her own words, used by her permission:

About 1933, I was on a campaign on Mersea Island, Essex, with Smith Wigglesworth. The day before he finished his campaign, he said, "Now, tomorrow night, I will just speak. You take the rest of the meeting. Find the hymns, read the lesson, do everything, and I will just do the speaking."

I spent a lot of time selecting hymns and the Scripture portion to be read. I felt this was important, because he was a very great man. I was only twenty-three; he was seventy-four.

We got to the meeting the next night, which was Sunday — and up he jumped. He always had his glasses on the end of his nose and sort of looked over the top.

He said, "We'll have a hymn," and we did. He said, "We'll pray," and he prayed. Then he said, "We'll have another hymn," and after that, he said, "We'll read a portion," and he took his New Testament out of his pocket.

I thought, "Oh, he has forgotten all about me leading the service and doing everything but the preaching. But I'm not going to remind him."

Then he said, "We'll have another hymn." We did, and when we got to the last two lines of the last verse, he turned to me and said, "You've got to preach next."

My legs turned to jelly, and my mind went blank. To this day, I cannot tell you a word of what I said.

Afterwards, he said to me in a rather gruff voice, "I'm going to 'roll you out' before I've finished with you."

"Why?" I asked. "What have I done?"

"It isn't what you've done; it is what you haven't done."

When I asked what he meant, he said, "Well, you can't run away and get ready when an emergency arises. The child of God is always ready. When I'm traveling by train and people know I am on that train, and it stops at a station even for five minutes, I'll go to the window, and they will say, 'Have you got a word from the Lord?'

"Of course I've got a word from the Lord. The child of God always has a word from the Lord. You've got to be ready, my girl. You can't run away and *get* ready. You've got to always *be* ready."

Dr. Serjeant went on to tell me of what she felt was one of her failures, a time when she did not put into practice what she had learned from Wigglesworth. A lady brought to her a little boy who had never walked. As Dr. Serjeant prayed for him, she felt the Lord definitely touch him and said so to his mother, who agreed.

Then the little boy said, "Mummy, I want to walk," but the mother picked him up, murmuring, "You will, darling, you will."

Dr. Serjeant did not confront the mother and confessed that at the time, she had not the courage. She later realized that she was not as ready as she should have been. She should have taken authority, commanded the mother to put down the child and let him walk. She continued:

> Brother Wigglesworth used to say, "You know, you can't treat the devil lightly. You have to be rough with him. You have to mean business. You must tell him with authority to come out. It's no use telling him a second time, because if you do, he knows you didn't meant it the first time. You have to have enough authority in the name of Jesus to command him to come out. In that name, he *must* come out.

When Smith Wigglesworth went to the Middle East to preach, his guide in Jerusalem was Tom Kemp, a missionary. Kemp has related what Wigglesworth did once to his interpreter, a government official who spoke classical Arabic. The man apparently was in some sort of bondage which brought a stiffness into the service the evangelist could not endure, and he decided to deal with it. He began to tell of a paralyzed man who had come to him for prayer.

As he spoke the words, "There was a man who was paralyzed, and I took hold of him like this," he turned, grabbed the interpreter by the throat, and said, "And I said, 'Loose him, and let him go.' "

The Spirit of God came on the interpreter, and he was liberated.

Wigglesworth said, "From then on, we had the freest meeting I have ever had in my life."

In the early days of the Pentecostal movement in Great Britain there were not many well-educated preachers in the move. They really knew God, but they did not know grammar!

This posed a problem for one couple who wanted to introduce an aristocratic friend to the wonderful truth of the fullness of the Spirit. However, they were afraid she would be distracted by uneducated speakers. Then a splendid opportunity presented itself. A convention was being held near their home, and the announced speakers were two godly men with first-class educations. They decided to take their friend to the meeting.

She went with them and heard a good word, but to the distress of her hosts, Smith Wigglesworth was there and said he had a message from the Lord. He gave it in his homespun style.

On the way home, this couple were hesitant to ask their guest her opinion of the service, but finally one of them did, and her reply surprised them.

"My dears, I thought those first two speakers were boring. But that old man! He had something, and I want it."

The reality of the Holy Spirit anointing had rested on his message, regardless of his style of speech and lack of grammar.

Wigglesworth may have been rough in his speech, but he was a man of his word. He promised one young man that he would come and help him if he ever needed help. Some time later, the young man wired that he did need help. Wigglesworth traveled at his own expense from the west coast of America to the east, from large crowds to a small, struggling group, because he had given his word.

He had asked God to help him never to exaggerate but to tell things as they really were. Those who knew him heard him repeat many incidents from his vast experience in illustration after illustration. They never heard his stories "grow." He never varied the facts.

It is said that a lady once came to the great evangelist Dwight L. Moody asking prayer to conquer exaggerating.

Moody responded, "Don't call it exaggeration. Call it by its proper name — lying." And that is also how Wigglesworth regarded embroidering or coloring incidents to make good stories.

He was outspoken about church membership methods. He did not believe in adding names just to increase the roll.

Quoting Acts 2:47, he would say, "Notice that the Lord added to the Church daily. If the Lord adds them, they'll be a blessing. But if you take in any that the Lord hasn't added, they'll be a nuisance. I would rather have the Lord build the church one by one than have half the town join it."

He had the same strong views regarding people holding office in a church. We were traveling home from a church once where he had held a meeting when suddenly, out of the blue, he said,

"They'll never have a revival in that church while they have that woman at the piano."

The pianist was gifted but overbearing. She ruled the service from the piano stool. I later shared with the pastor what Wigglesworth had said, but he rejected it. That lady stayed at the piano for twenty-five years, and they never had even the slightest breath of revival.

There was no pretense about Smith Wigglesworth. He was boldly straightforward because he wanted to strip away from the Church all that was a sham. His heart was set on revival, and he knew that cleansing and obedience were vital to the manifestation of the presence and power of the Lord.

Chapter 4:

A Heart of Compassion

Wigglesworth's rough methods and blunt speech hid a heart that was full of compassion. While staying in a missionary home in what was then Palestine, he met an "upper class" lady who argued the superiority of her class. Wigglesworth, on the other hand, was very much for the working man.

When the discussion got too warm, he would stop and say, "I want to pray." He did, with tears, and the lady told Tom Kemp, "When I saw his tears and felt his heart throb for the needy, I knew that he was a man of God. It changed my attitude toward him."

I had my office in my home in those days, and many times I would be interrupted by Brother Wigglesworth, asking me to come and help him pray over requests that had reached him by mail. When he read these to me before prayer, he would comment on the sad cases brought to his attention. When he prayed, it was often with strong crying — weeping over people he had never met.

I experienced this compassion personally when I was invited to be one of the speakers at the Preston Easter Convention one year. This was one of the largest Pentecostal conventions in Great Britain. Some of the other speakers were of international renown, and at the time, I was a mere beginner on the "convention circuit." These and other factors put me under considerable stress.

Wigglesworth discerned this in the ministers' room before the first meeting. When the other preachers had gone to take their places on the platform, he turned to me, and in such a gentle, gracious manner, said, "Brother, you'll be the first speaker after I — by and through the operation of the Holy Spirit — have opened the door as wide as possible." He laid his hand on my shoulder and prayed for me.

Within ten minutes, I was on my feet delivering my first message in the full liberty of the Spirit.

Esther Horton, wife of a pastor and a friend of ours, told us the following incident:

> I took a friend crippled with rheumatoid arthritis to hear Brother Wigglesworth speak. After his message, he called the sick forward for prayer. Because of her crippled condition, my friend was still at the back of the hall when the others who had gone forward had reached the front.
>
> Wigglesworth looked up, saw my friend struggling, and called to her to stand still. He said, "Sister, the trial of your faith is as gold." Turning to the congregation, he said, "We don't even need to minister to our sister. She's receiving healing now."
>
> His compassion overflowed in his voice. He wept as he prayed, and the healing virtue of Jesus ministered life to my friend. She didn't need to go to the front of the church for healing, but she ran forward to show that she was healed.

Another incident that at first glance seems far removed from compassion comes to my mind as I write. When Wigglesworth was chairman of a large meeting, one of the speakers had just returned from a visit to the mission field, and he became very intense. The longer he spoke, the more intense and emotional he became until the atmosphere was growing unbearable. The congregation got more and more uncomfortable by the minute.

Then Wigglesworth stood up, moved just behind the speaker, and quietly said, "Sit down, brother, you're killing yourself *and* us."

Turning to the congregation, he said, "We'll sing a hymn, while our brother gets quiet."

When the song was finished, he told the preacher, "Go on now, and go quieter."

The speaker was a very godly man with much grace, and he accepted the rebuke of his chairman. He learned a valuable lesson from this astonishing experience and came to see it as a revelation of the compassion as well as the strength of Brother Wigglesworth — compassion for the speaker as well as for the congregation!

The Lord does not pour compassion into us the way we pour gasoline into our cars. It is released in our spirits as we are filled with the Holy Spirit and dwell continually in the presence of Jesus. That means being filled with God. Wigglesworth's frequent prayer was to be emptied of self and filled with God.

The mainspring of his compassion was to feel as Christ felt.

Chapter 5:

Simplicity: A Defense Against Temptation

Wigglesworth was a simple man — I do not mean simple-minded nor simplistic. He was far from that, having a very sharp, clear mind. However, he was uncomplicated. His faith was simple and strong. He considered nothing impossible because he simply believed God's Word. Apparently, he originated the often-repeated saying: "God says it; I believe it; and that settles it!"

He was free from distraction because he did not multiply possessions. He did not seek or need an affluent lifestyle but lived for Jesus. This was one of his strengths and a defense against every temptation. His simplicity was in his absolute obedience to God, his lack of ambiguity. Consequently, Satan in all his craftiness, could not take him by surprise.

It seems he was guided by two things in his relationship to God:

1. What endangers my relationship with Jesus?
2. What would the Lord have me do?

Other people could have hobbies, read books, and listen to music, but for him these were distracting things. If he was in the company of Christians who were engaged in any of these things, he passed no judgment on them. In a gracious and kindly way, he would just say, "If you don't mind, I'll go to my room and pray."

He sought earnestly to ascertain God's will, and when he found it, he unhesitatingly carried it out. Jesus really was his Lord. He retained his simplicity by a moment by moment walk with Jesus. He had eyes for Jesus only and saw others only through those eyes. When out walking, he would be worshipping. When he was being driven by car, frequently he would be heard murmuring, "Lovely Jesus."

For Wigglesworth, there were no "unnecessary necessities" — just faith and apostolic simplicity. He was totally open to God so that the life and energy of the Spirit flowed through him without hindrance.

His Generosity Was Based on Faith

Many thousands of pounds — when the English pound was worth $4 or $5 — were given to Smith Wigglesworth. He could have been a very wealthy man; however, he kept only enough to minister to his simple needs. The rest he gave away to missions and to the needy.

Harold Womersley, later an outstanding missionary to Zaire, was a driver for Wigglesworth on some of his meetings in England. One thing that impressed him greatly was that Wigglesworth always gave him, just a young candidate for the mission field and "chauffeur" for the well-known evangelist, half of whatever honorarium he received.

In America, Wigglesworth saw for the first time the practice of taking up "love offerings" to meet a visiting speaker's needs. This kind of offering was unknown in England at the time.

Sometimes when he was conducting a long series of meetings, more than one such offering would be suggested. Usually, he declined — unless the folks were willing for him to give the extra offering to missions.

His special joy at the time was to give to what was then called Congo Evangelistic Mission, founded in the heart of the African continent by his son-in-law, Jimmy Salter, and noted missionary Willie Burton. On one occasion, he received a large check, but hearing of the need of a couple longing to get back to their mission field, he endorsed the check and gave it to them.

As in all things, he was very practical in following the commands of Scripture. He lived by faith in Christ. Yet living by faith did not mean going around acting like a pauper. He bought good clothes, because they were more economical. He felt a Christian should honor the Lord in his appearance. He did not choose the cheapest way to travel because it was more physically draining, and he knew he had to be fit for a demanding ministry schedule.

He said, "I'm not saving the Lord's money; I'm saving the Lord's servant." But he was careful not to carry this to the extreme.

So convinced was he of the Lord's sufficient supply that on one occasion he is reported to have said, "If the Lord doesn't look after me, it will be time to go back to plumbing."

At this time, there was a splendid generation of men and women who lived by faith, among them Wigglesworth, Burton, Salter, and their good friend Howard Carter.

Someone once said to Carter, "You must have had some hard times, living by faith."

"Hard times!" replied Carter. "My brother, that would not be *living* by faith; it would be *dying* by faith."

When Wigglesworth learned to give, he was released from bondage. He moved from this world's economy to God's economy.

Victory After Severe Battles

Wigglesworth was a holy and righteous man in his later years, but he had not always been self-controlled. He had severe battles in the earlier days of his life and ministry, but he pressed through to God for victory. At one time, he had a violent temper and sought earnestly to conquer it. John Carter, whom I referred to earlier, sent me this report in Wigglesworth's own words, as he told it once in a meeting in Switzerland:

I used to have a tremendous temper, even going white with passion. My whole nature was outside God that way. But God knew His child could never be of service to the world unless he was wholly sanctified.

I was difficult to please at the table. My wife was a good cook, but there always was something wrong. After God sanctified me, I heard her testify in a meeting that from that time I was pleased with everything.

She said, "I never saw such a change in a man."

(Also) I had men working for me. I wanted to be a good testimony to them. After I was sanctified, one day they waited for me after work and said, "We would like the spirit you have."

The Spirit of God can change our nature. His Word is creative, and as you believe, the creative power will change your whole nature. You cannot reach this attitude, except by faith. No man can keep himself. The God of almightiness spreads His covering over you, saying, "I am able to do all things. All things are possible to him that believeth." (Mark 9:23.)

If Christian perfection is perfect love, as John Wesley defined it, then this question of temper can be the acid test of our spirituality. Not only temper in its outbursts, but temper in its touchiness. Smith Wigglesworth encourages us all by his experience of deliverance. There is victory over temper, moods, temperament, and every alien thing that would rob us of God's best in our lives.

The secret lies in allowing Jesus to reign in our hearts. For Wigglesworth, that meant ten days of earnest, determined seeking of God's face. It was then, he said, that God dealt with the "Wigglesworth nature" and worked in him the Jesus nature.

Chapter 6:

An Emphasis on Life

*O*ne day I offered him a beautiful rosebud to wear. He declined it quite strongly.

"No, thank you, Brother. As soon as that rose was cut from the bush, it began to die. I don't want any death on me."

Walking down the road one day, he remarked that in the south of England most houses had tiled roofs, while in the north slate was used. He called tiled roofs "dead." The life is baked out of them, he said, and he preferred slate roofs because they were living stone. His emphasis always was life!

Because he had to begin work in a woolen mill when he was seven years old, Wigglesworth had little formal education. He did not learn to read until after he married Mary Jane Featherstone, whom he and everyone else called "Polly." They were married in 1882 and had five children. For years, she was the minister, and he helped while building a successful plumbing business.

Polly taught him to read, "but," said he, "she never taught me to spell!" He would no doubt have appreciated President Grover Cleveland's remark that it is a poor kind of mind that can think of only one way to spell a word.

He was ministering in our church once on Mark 11:23: "He shall have whatsoever he saith," when he asked the congregation, "Have you begun to 'saith' yet?"

For twenty minutes, he spoke about "saithing." At home after the service, I said, "You know, Brother Wigglesworth, you can't *saith*."

He replied, "If you can't *saith*, you don't know God!"

I persisted, "It is 'I say, you say, he saith.'"

"You've got it," said Wigglesworth, "hang onto it!"

But I pressed my point, "Your grammar is wrong."

Wigglesworth replied, "I don't know much about grammar, but if you can't *saith*, get down on your knees until you can."

When a young man challenged Dwight L. Moody, "I don't like your grammar, Mr. Moody," the great evangelist quickly replied, "Young man, I'm using all the grammar I have for God. What are you doing with yours?"

And J. W. Robertson, an outstanding British preacher, said, "It is not the possession of extraordinary gifts that makes extraordinary usefulness, but the dedication of what we have to God."

That was Wigglesworth's secret. He was wholly yielded to God, and all there was of him could be used by God. One sunny day in our peaceful garden, we were discussing a criticism both of us had seen about Christians who went forward frequently at the end of services.

Some thought it indicated insecurity, which perhaps it did. Yet Wigglesworth saw something important in it, saying, "Every fresh revelation calls for a new dedication."

He perceived that while we have made, or should have made, once and for all a consecration of our lives to God, there will be all along the way further unveilings of the Lord, of His power, and of His purposes. As each fuller revelation comes into view, we commit ourselves afresh to God for its fulfillment in our lives. (Rom. 12:1,2.)

Chapter 7:

A Man of One Book

To Wigglesworth, the Word of God was so precious he carried it in his heart, and he carried a copy of at least the New Testament everywhere he went. He even offered a reward to anyone who found him without a portion of the Scripture on his person.

You could not be with him long before you discovered two things:

First, he had an overmastering love for the Word, and secondly, he had an absolute confidence in the God of the Word. Because he loved God's Word, he read it; because he read it, he had faith; because he had faith, he acted; and because he acted, his faith grew. For this reason, he was "a man of one book," a phrase coined by John Wesley.

Wesley was well-educated, one of the best-read men of his day. After reading widely, he came to see the Bible as utterly unrivaled, the book above all other books, hence his longing and determination to major in the Bible and to be a "man of one book."

Wigglesworth, as I have mentioned before, had a very limited education. After he learned to read, he made a deliberate choice to limit his reading to the Bible. He told me that, because he learned to read so late, he felt he should keep that ability for the reading of the supreme book.

At one stage, Wigglesworth even advised young ministers to burn their libraries. Donald Gee, a widely traveled and honored Bible teacher, told me he had to go around comforting and counseling those who had taken Wigglesworth at his word — and later regretted it.

Frankly, I do not think he meant his words to be taken literally. By overemphasis, he was stressing the priority and indispensability of God's own Word for preachers. Some people criticized him for inconsistency because, while advising others not to read books, he authored two — *Ever Increasing Faith* and *Faith That Prevails.*

He would reply with a smile, "I didn't write those books. Someone took down my sermons in shorthand and then published them."

One of the reasons for Wigglesworth's high esteem for the Word was its cleansing power. He believed deeply the need for being spiritually clean.

He told his grandson, "Leslie, if I read the newspaper I come out dirtier than I went in. If I read my Bible, I come out cleaner than I went in, and I like being clean!"

You never needed a devotional book when Wigglesworth stayed with you. After every meal, he would say something like this, "Well, we've fed our bodies. Now we must feed our souls." Then out would come his Bible. He would read a portion, then comment on it, as God had spoken to him that very day. Then he would illustrate what he was saying with some vivid experience from his ministry. After every meal he shared with us, we rose from the table satisfied physically and also with a glow in our souls.

An American lady missionary ran a missionary home in Ramalah, Palestine (now Israel), and she was a strict disciplinarian. A missionary living there at the time Wigglesworth visited told me, "You went to bed at a certain time. You got up at a certain time. You sat down to breakfast on time. You finished on time. You rose from the table on time."

This did not suit Wigglesworth, and he told the lady, "Sister, this won't do. We must take time to listen to Father. You will do more work in less time and with less strain if you listen to Father first."

He insisted on reading the Word, then commenting on it, following that with prayer. Tom Kemp, who reported this, said this practice changed the atmosphere of the home.

"There was a sense of sweetness that persisted even after Wigglesworth had left," Kemp said.

Wigglesworth had bestowed blessing through the Word.

One day, I tried an experiment, asking Wigglesworth if he would like me to read to him.

"What do you want to read?" he asked.

I suggested a sermon by the great 19th century preacher Charles H. Spurgeon, whose last years as pastor of London's Metropolitan Tabernacle spanned Wigglesworth's young manhood. Wigglesworth was not enthusiastic, but he allowed me to try. So I began to read Spurgeon's sermon on the crucifixion. He talked so tenderly about the cross that Wigglesworth began quietly to weep.

However, as I moved to Spurgeon's second main point, it was only a short while until Wigglesworth exclaimed, "Stop it! He's missed it" — and he had! That ended my attempts to read books to Wigglesworth. But he would listen untiringly if you read to him from the Bible.

He had a conviction that if you did not have a hunger for righteousness as revealed in God's Word, you were not in the place God wanted you to be. You needed an insatiable appetite for the Scripture of truth, he thought, otherwise you missed God's plan.

This was his belief:

> If it is in the Bible, it is so. It's not even to be prayed about. It's to be received and acted upon. Inactivity is a robber which steals blessings. Increase comes by action, by using what we have and know. Your life must be one of going on from faith to faith.[1]

This belief he applied to everything — holiness, witnessing, baptism in water and in the Spirit, and divine healing. For example, if you asked him for a good book on divine healing, most likely he would reply, "What's wrong with the Bible?"

He believed that by prayer and the revelation of the Holy Spirit the simplest believer could understand the Word of God.

He had a saying, "Some people like to read their Bibles in the Hebrew; some like to read it in the Greek; I like to read it in the Holy Spirit."

Consequently, he had some remarkable insights into the Scriptures.

One day he said to me, "Brother, God wants all He's got in you."

When I asked him what he meant, he said, "You'll find it in James."

So I read the Epistle of James more than once, but found nothing like what Wigglesworth had said. Finally, I read James

---

[1]Frodsham, Stanley. *Smith Wigglesworth — Apostle of Faith* (Springfield: Gospel Publishing House, 1948), p. 111.

on my knees praying, "Lord, show me what Wigglesworth is trying to tell me."

I came to a halt at James 4:5:

> Do ye think that the scripture saith in vain, The spirit that dwelleth in us lusteth to envy?

Even that did not seem to say what Wigglesworth had said. Prayerfully I began to study with the help of what Greek scholarship was within my reach. I discovered that this passage is saying that God has a passionate desire for a full response from the Spirit He has placed in us.

This was confirmed by other versions of the New Testament that were published long after Wigglesworth's death. God longs intensely for unhindered communication and total response between Him and the believer indwelt by the Spirit.

This is a profound explanation of a verse which, in the *King James Version*, is extremely difficult. How did Wigglesworth arrive at this interpretation, which later was confirmed by scholarly translators? He found it because he read his Bible in the Holy Spirit.

That does not mean we should despise scholarship. Far from it! We would not have the Bible in our own language without scholars. But it does mean that by prayer, meditation, and diligence — all under the anointing of the Holy Spirit — our renewed minds and spirits can discern the hidden truths of God's precious Word. (Eph. 4:23, Col. 3:10.)

The well-known 18th century preacher Dr. G. Campbell Morgan was a Bible scholar of the first order, but even his view of a Bible verse was surpassed by that of an old lady he was visiting. She was dying, and Dr. Morgan read to her Jesus' words in Matthew 28:20, "Lo, I am with you alway."

Then he said, "Isn't that a wonderful promise?"

"Sir," replied the woman, "that isn't a promise — it's a fact!"

A deep reverence for God's Word is not "bibliolatry," but a recognition of the divine source and amounts to worship for the Author. Our respect for the holy Scripture also should extend to the public reading of it. One preacher I heard called the people to stand to honor God's Word as he read, but then he garbled the reading so badly it was difficult to follow its meaning.

Another preacher rarely read the Bible publicly without interpolating the reading with his own comments. Preachers should concentrate on an unadulterated, uninterpreted, meaningful, Spirit-anointed public reading of the Scripture. Expounding on it can come later. The Bible then will come alive to their congregations.

I heard one lady say to a preacher, "I want to thank you for the way you read Romans 6 tonight. I had never understood it until I heard you read it."

The Word truly came alive when Wigglesworth read it. He *was* a "man of one book."

Chapter 8:

Faith: The Key to Wigglesworth's Ministry

*S*mith Wigglesworth many times was called "the apostle of faith" because he believed God unequivocably.

Many today use the title "apostle" very freely and loosely, when it needs safeguarding. Even the Apostle Paul was careful in his use of the term. In Romans 1:1, he said he was *called* to be an apostle. In Second Corinthians 12:11, he said he was nothing behind the chiefest of apostles, and in First Corinthians 15:9, he said he was "least" of all the apostles and was not "meet" to be called an apostle.

Obviously he viewed the title differently at various times in his life, but the marks of an apostle — the reality that is more than a name — were ever present. (2 Cor. 12:12.)

Wigglesworth also recognized that it is not the title you have, nor the gift you claim, but the manifestation of the power of God that counts. (1 Cor. 1:31.) The manifestation of the power of God was shown in his life through faith.

Seeing the evidence of his faith, we are moved to ask, "Is such a faith within my reach? Can I possess 'like precious faith'?"

I trust this chapter will help and encourage those true seekers after that kind of faith. I have two important observations to make concerning such faith:

First, Wigglesworth did not arrive at his degree of faith in one leap. He reached it by a process of failure and success. Whoever you are, whatever situation you are in, however weak your faith is at this moment, *your faith can grow.*

Secondly, Wigglesworth believed that *God has no favorites.* He believed *all* Christians have the potential to grow into strong faith. This matter of favorites was illustrated quite sweetly for us by a Swiss friend of my wife's named Martha.

In broken English, she said one day, "I was cross with Jesus because He had favorites, and I told Him so. He asked me why I said that, and I told Him, 'Because you let John lean on your bosom.' Do you know what Jesus said? He said, 'Martha, *all* the disciples could have leaned on My bosom. Only John wanted to.' "

Every believer can have enough faith for the fulfillment of God's will in his or her life. Wigglesworth had a noble concept of God's plan for him and was determined to seek God for the faith required to exercise his ministry.

Not all will have the same calling; not all will need the same dramatic faith. But all Christians have the potential for the gifts of the Spirit to operate through them, and all Christians can possess faith for the effective exercise of whatever gift He chooses to operate through them.

William Hacking, a pastor in the north of England, had Wigglesworth in his church for meetings. One day some of the young men of his church, soul-winning young men, accompanied the evangelist on a walk.

He said, "Well, young men, you can ask me any question you like, and I'll answer it best as I can."

One of them asked the inevitable question, "Mr. Wigglesworth, how can we come to possess great faith?"

"Now, listen," said Wigglesworth, "here is the answer: 'First the blade, then the ear, after that the full corn in the ear.' Mark 4:28."

Wigglesworth saw three degrees of faith. The first degree is *saving* faith. All who receive Jesus as Savior have received that faith. This faith is seed that, nourished by hearing the Word of God, can grow:

> For by grace are ye saved through faith; and that not of yourselves: it is the gift of God.
>
> Ephesians 2:8

The second degree he saw was *the faith of the Lord Jesus.* In Galatians 2:20, Wigglesworth saw that it was the faith *of* the Lord Jesus being spoken of, not faith *in* the Son of God. It is Christ's own faith imparted to His children:

> I am crucified with Christ: nevertheless, I live; yet not I, but Christ liveth in me: and the life which I now live in the flesh I live by the faith *of* the Son of God, who loved me, and gave himself for me.

Thirdly, he said, there is the *gift of faith:*

> But the manifestation of the Spirit is given to every man to profit withal . . . to another faith by the same Spirit.
>
> 1 Corinthians 12:7,9

There were those who quibbled over these distinctions, but Wigglesworth blithely ignored their quibbles and went on demonstrating he had a faith that glorified God in practical results.

Faith that saves is a faith that works. Faith that achieves is a faith that acts. (James 2:18-20.)

For Wigglesworth, there was one thing more: He pressed through by faith in the Word of God to faith in the God of the Word. There *is* a distinction. Romans 4:3 says that Abraham believed *God*. The Apostle Paul did not write that Abraham believed *about* God nor even believed *in* God. Abraham believed God as a Person.

It follows inevitably that if you believe God as a Person, you will believe every word that He speaks. Faith in God Himself is direct contact with God. It is a confidence that inspires action.

For Smith Wigglesworth, Hebrews 12:2, "Looking unto Jesus the author and finisher of our faith," meant unbroken communion with Jesus, dwelling deeply in the presence of the Lord. As he gazed on Jesus, his faith grew, and he was changed from glory to glory. (2 Cor. 3:18.) That same place of abiding, that same privilege of gazing on the Lord, is open to us!

He believed that faith means action. Once while preaching, he said, "If there is anything in your heart in the way of condemnation, you cannot pray the prayer of faith. Purity is vital to faith. How is faith received? It is received by your acting with what you now have. If you act with what you have, your faith will be increased. You can never increase faith but by acting."

Once a lady wrote a long letter to Wigglesworth telling about her problems and quoting a large number of scriptures.

He sent the letter back to her with these words written on it, "Believe your own letter."

She did — and was healed. In other words, she *acted* on what she already had.

Praying for the Sick

He told me of the first time he ever prayed for the sick. It was during the time he and Polly were operating a mission in Bradford, Yorkshire. Wigglesworth heard of a meeting in Leeds, nine miles away, where they prayed for the sick. Each week, he took people there from his mission to be prayed for, and miracles took place.

One day, the leader of the meeting said, "Brother Wigglesworth, I have to be away next week, so you must take the meeting."

"I can't!" said Wigglesworth, "I have never prayed for the sick."

The leader replied, "God has shown me that you are the one to take the meeting. You must do it."

When he arrived the next week, there was no one else to take charge, so he did his best. This is what he told me:

> I don't know what I preached, but I do remember that when I called for the sick, about twelve people came forward for prayer. The first was a large-framed man leaning on two sticks. As soon as I touched that man, the power of God hit him. He dropped his sticks; he started to jump; then he started to run, and ran all around the place. The faith of the others — *and* mine — was so quickened that everyone I prayed for that day was healed.

Wigglesworth saw it as God's compassion, helping him in a time of need, and helping his faith to grow. He began in trembling and fear, but he acted on what faith he had, and God honored his acting in faith.

John Wesley taught his preachers, "Preach faith until you have it, and then because you have it, you will preach faith."

Faith is reciprocal — act in faith, and you will have greater faith. So many people, seeing Wigglesworth in his later ministry forgot, or most likely never knew of, his early struggles.

He knew poverty and hard work, even as a youngster of six beginning to work in the turnip fields by 6 a.m. and staying at it for ten to twelve hours. But from a child, he was determined to know God, "precept upon precept; line upon line" (Is. 28:10).

He said, "Great faith is the product of great fights. Great testimonies are the outcome of great tests. Great triumphs can only come out of great trials."[1]

The tests he went through led him to a simple, basic faith startling in its simplicity. He had such confidence in God that he took him at His Word. Consequently, he was not moved by human opinion. He knew the danger spoken of by the Lord:

> How can ye believe, which received honor one of another, and seek not the honor that cometh from God only?
>
> John 5:44

Wigglesworth knew that Hebrews 12:2 — Jesus is the "author and finisher of our faith" — was the basis of "New Testament faith," faith based on total trust in Jesus. That is the faith that supported the early Christians, the faith that Wigglesworth had, and the faith we need today.

---

[1] *Apostle of Faith.* p. 135.

Chapter 9:

New Testament Faith

*F*aith is not mental acquiescence, nor even the ability to count a thing done. It is the deep awareness imparted by Jesus that a certain thing *is* done.

Early in his ministry, Wigglesworth was called to pray for a young woman who obviously was demon-possessed. He went into the home, and the woman's husband was there with the baby. When they tried to bring the baby to the woman to nurse, she flung herself away. Wigglesworth was moved deeply with compassion. He knew the situation was desperate and needed desperate remedy.

He got on his face before God, and his faith was quickened. He began to penetrate the heavens. He saw in the presence of God the limitations of his own faith. As he tarried there, another faith came to him, a faith that could not be denied. He came back from that experience of the immediate presence of God a changed man.

With authority, he commanded the demons to come out of her. The young lady rolled over in bed and went to sleep for fourteen hours. Then she woke completely free.

This "storming of heaven" (spiritual warfare) was vital in his view. By it, Wigglesworth pressed through into the presence of God against every satanic attempt to hinder.

He gazed on Jesus, and his faith grew strong. He had eyes for Jesus only. He communed with Him through the Word, through prayer, through speaking with other tongues. His faith was not a formula, but came of discipline, through "pressing through." (Heb. 4:11, 10:20.)

The real issue is that, for Smith Wigglesworth, faith flowed out of a relationship with Jesus.

I once asked him if the Holy Spirit operated the "gift of faith" listed in First Corinthians 12:9 through him, and his reply was, "It is not for me to claim that I have a gift. If I have it, the manifestation of it will be the evidence that it is there. It's not what I claim, but what God does."

He saw danger in claiming a gift or a title. It could cause people to look to the person through whom the gift operates rather than at the true Giver of the gift to the Body, to look at the instrument rather than the One who is using the instrument. Then there may be the temptation to get into pride or to move into areas not of God's choosing. Furthermore, he saw that a man could lose touch with God and be left with an empty title.

Let me conclude this chapter with the account of some unusual demonstrations of faith.

Faith in Operation

The Rev. J. E. Stiles, an Assemblies of God minister and author, had a remarkable ministry of leading people into the baptism in the Holy Spirit. This ministry began when he saw and heard Wigglesworth minister in California at a large camp meeting.

To a large company of people gathered that night, Wigglesworth taught two lessons on faith. First, he asked all those who had not received the baptism in the Spirit to stand. Then he asked all those who had been baptized but not spoken in tongues for at least six months to stand. Finally, he called all of the several hundred people standing to come forward and crowd around the pulpit.

"Now," said Wigglesworth, "I'm going to teach you the first lesson in faith. You will speak with tongues by faith. I want you to lift your hands and press forward."

When everyone did, he said, "I'm going to pray a simple prayer. When I've finished, I'll say, 'Go,' and you will all speak in tongues."

Stiles said to the man standing next to him, "This might work in Britain, but it will never work here."

The next thing he heard was Wigglesworth praying. Then he heard him say, "Go!" To his astonishment, the next sound was like that of many waters. Everyone was praising God in tongues, "and," said Stiles, "I myself was speaking louder than anyone else."

Presently, Wigglesworth cried, "Hold it!" in stentorian tones. Things quietened down, but a few people kept speaking in tongues. Again he said, "Hold it!" Finally all was quiet. Then he told them he was going to teach them the second lesson on faith, and that was how to sing in the Spirit by faith.

He commanded them to press forward again and raise their hands. They did.

He said, "I'm going to pray a simple prayer. When I've finished, I'll say, 'Go!' and you will all begin to sing in tongues by faith."

Again Stiles demurred, saying, "That cannot happen. The other did happen, but not this. He hasn't given us any tune. We don't know what to sing. It will be utter confusion."

But Stiles said that when the evangelist prayed, then said, "Go! Sing!" the sound was like a vast glorious choir. The group sang in perfect harmony and at other times in unison. He said it seemed as if there were solos, sometimes groups, and sometimes a full choir, all under the baton of the greatest conductor. He had never heard anything like it.

Stiles said he learned a bigger lesson than speaking and singing in tongues by faith. He learned that the Holy Spirit operates on faith, and from that moment, he was launched on a ministry of faith which extended throughout the United States and Canada, a ministry that saw thousands baptized in the Spirit by faith.

A few years ago, I met a daughter of J. E. Stiles, who confirmed to me this story.

One day Wigglesworth was being shown around a farm by the owner, a dear friend. Visiting one field, he commented on the beauty of it. But his friend said, "It's not what it looks. The whole field is ruined by blight."

Wigglesworth lifted his heart to God. Faith flowed in, and he stretched out his hand over the field in the name of Jesus. The field was completely cleansed of blight and the entire crop was saved. In fact, that was the best crop his friend had from any field!

A lady with advanced cancer asked Wigglesworth to pray for her. He went to her home with James Salter, his son-in-law, and they prayed. She was immediately and gloriously delivered. Later, as she cleaned out a closet, she came across an old Bible that she had not seen in twelve years.

Glancing through it, she saw that years before she had underlined part of Isaiah 58:8, "Thine health shall spring forth speedily." She realized that God had spoken to her all those years ago, but she had never actuated her faith. She could have been spared those years of suffering.

Bishop Ronald Coady and his wife were ministering in New South Wales, Australia, in 1950 where they met a Methodist deaconess called "Sister Mary." She brought them large quantities of tracts to use in their crusades.

While there, they were reading Stanley Frodsham's book, *Smith Wigglesworth — Apostle of Faith*. The incident of his raising a young woman from the dead especially had gripped them, and when Sister Mary came in, they read it to her, adding, "How we should love to meet that lady!"

She said, "You know that lady."

They protested that they did not, but she persisted, "You've known her for some time. I am that lady."

The three of them laughed together with holy joy at God's "coincidences." She then told them of being paralyzed from the waist down in 1922 and of being seriously ill. Wigglesworth was holding meetings in her town, and her friends urged her to let them take her to a meeting for prayer. However, she did not believe in divine healing and did not wish to be prayed for.

She soon became worse and, in fact, was dying. Her friends asked if she would allow the evangelist to pray for her if they brought him to the house. She finally consented, but he was delayed. Before he arrived, she died.

Sister Mary Pople related that she went to Heaven and was allowed in the throne room. She saw the Lord Jesus sitting on His throne. She saw light such as she had never seen and heard music such as she had never heard. Her heart was filled with rapturous joy.

As she looked at the Lord, He pointed to the doorway by which she had entered, and she knew she had to go back even if she did not want to. When she went through that door, she heard a voice that later she knew was Smith Wigglesworth's.

He was saying, "Death, I rebuke you in the name of Jesus."

Then he commanded Mary to live. Her eyes opened, and those who had been weeping around her bed began to rejoice. She arose and dressed, and there was a knock at the door. Some girls from her Bible study group had arrived, thinking she was dead. To their surprise and joy, Mary herself opened the door to them. She continued in the Lord's service for many years. Not only was she raised from the dead, but she was totally healed of her sickness that had been unto death and of the paralysis that had bound her for years.

Without faith, it is impossible to please Him.

Hebrews 11:6

Chapter 10:

Sanctification: Unbroken Communion With God

I heard American author-pastor-teacher Judson Cornwall say once concerning Smith Wigglesworth:

> I will never forget the sense of awe I felt at the authority that man had. It was an absolutely glorious, positive authority in God. He knew the voice of his God. He knew what God was about to do, and he was always there at the right time when God did it. He had the ability to speak it just as God did it; or, as he spoke it, God did it.

The secret lay, I believe, in the large degree to which Wigglesworth had entered into the inmost life of the Lord Jesus as revealed in John 5:19,20. Jesus said in those verses that He did nothing on earth that He had not seen the Father do in heaven. That is an increasing revelation.

Perhaps the emphasis on the miraculous in Wigglesworth's life and ministry has obscured to a large extent his insistent call for holy living.

Kathleen Chambers, daughter of Oswald Chambers, heard a great deal about holiness in her home when she was a small girl. One day, while playing with a rag doll, she tried to make it stand up. Its limp rag legs collapsed every time.

In disgust, she exclaimed, "He ain't 'sankified' yet!"

That is sadly true of many oft-collapsing Christians! However, what joy there is in true holiness. The pure in heart see God. Samuel Chadwick said:

> Holiness brings the soul into fellowship with the redeeming Son of God. When believers rejoice in its possession, sinners are awakened and saved.[1]

The truth of the great prayer of the writer of Hebrews needs to be experienced by us all:

> Now the God of peace, that brought again from the dead our Lord Jesus, that great shepherd of the sheep, through the blood of the everlasting covenant,
>
> Make you perfect in every good work to do his will, working in you that which is well-pleasing in his sight, through Jesus Christ; to whom be glory forever and ever, Amen.
>
> Hebrews 13:20,21

There is a winsomeness in the Greek word *katartizo* translated "make you perfect":

In Matthew 21:16, it means to set in order as in music.

In Galatians 6:1, it is translated "restore" and carries the idea of putting back in place a dislocated limb.

In First Thessalonians 3:10, it means to supply what is "lacking."

In Hebrews 11:3, it is translated "framed" and implies setting in order as in a machine.

In Matthew 4:21, the translation is "mending." This carried a double idea: repairing what was broken and arranging for future use.

---

[1]Chadwick, Samuel. *The Call of Christian Perfection*, (London: Epworth Press, 1936), p. 90.

In Ephesians 4:11,12, the thought is of equipping for service.

Wigglesworth achieved the goal of holiness because he determined not to settle for anything less. He "prayed through." His experience of "sanctification by faith" was fundamental to his later life and ministry. Teachers in the "holiness movement" called it the baptism in the Spirit, and so did he at first.

Later, he came to see what the true baptism in the Spirit is, but he never denied his earlier experience. It was an essential part of God's plan. For the rest of his life, he associated holiness and power.

Wigglesworth lived *so* close to God in the last years of his ministry. He dwelt in the secret place of the Most High. *Unbroken communion* best describes his relationship with God. In that intimacy, he entered deeply into the experience of Jesus. He, too, saw what God did in heaven, then in Jesus' name, he did it on earth.

Comparatively few dwell where he dwelt. It is an "awe-full" place. Isaiah expressed this vividly in Isaiah 33:14:

Who among us shall dwell with the devouring fire? Who among us shall dwell with everlasting burnings?

David asked the same question in Psalm 24:3,4.

Wigglesworth knew that without holiness, no man can see the Lord (Heb. 12:14), so with all his heart, he sought holiness. There was no "shilly-shallying," no playing games, no pretense. He meant to *see* God. (Matt. 5:8.) One of his great joys in the baptism of the Holy Spirit was the sense of cleansing. He had a vision of an empty cross and Jesus glorified. He cried out in ecstasy, "Clean, clean, clean."

His Life in the Spirit

His life in the Spirit began with the certainty of the new birth he experienced as a young boy. Yet he felt that was not all there was to a relationship with God. He was eager to grow spiritually. A few months after his fourteenth birthday, when he was confirmed in the Church of England with the bishop laying hands on him, he was filled with an overwhelming joy. Afterwards, he came to believe this was the beginning of the work of the Holy Spirit in his life that culminated in the baptism of the Spirit nearly forty years later.

Yet even that was not enough. As he grew older, he came to realize that he had to face up to temptation and defeat in his Christian walk. Perhaps, as we have already seen, his greatest weakness was his temper.

His temper was at times all-consuming. He would go pale and shake with rage over sometimes trivial matters, almost losing control.

Also, there was a period in his life when he turned almost completely from their mission ministry to business. A plumber by trade, he became very busy and successful. He and his employees worked from early morning until late at night, and he began to prosper greatly. As a result, his private devotions and church attendance suffered.

His love for Jesus, prayer, the Word, and the fellowship of believers lessened until he was gripped by materialism. In the meantime, Polly increased in spiritual fervor. As he grew colder, she grew hotter. This irritated him. One night, when she was very late returning from a service, he said to her in a severe tone, "This must stop."

She said, "Smith, you're my husband, but Jesus is my Lord."

This angered him so much that he put her out the front door and locked her out. But he had forgotten that the back door was unlocked. She ran around the house and came in the other door laughing. He could not resist her laughter and joined in. That was the beginning of his restoration.

He said to himself, "This won't do in a child of God," and he determined to meet God at every opportunity. Setting aside ten days, he presented his body a living sacrifice. (Rom. 12:1,2.) He prayed, wept, soaked in the Word, and pleaded the promises. He faced up to the cross until he began to understand what Paul meant in Galatians 2:20.

This is how he described the experience to me: "God worked the old Wigglesworth-nature out and began to work the new Jesus-nature in."

The transformation was obvious to all who knew him. He became the calmest, purest man I ever knew. What he taught after that, he lived. His grandson, Leslie Wigglesworth, saw him in the relaxed environment of family life, and he bears witness that he never saw him moody or out of sorts.

Wigglesworth's failure at that point in his life was real. His sin was real, but it brought him to the end of himself and caused him to cry mightily unto God. He reached the place of brokenness. Such brokenness may well be the prerequisite of full spiritual development.

He faced the love of business and consequent love of money that took him away from God for a while.

He faced his almost uncontrollable temper, surrendering it to Jesus until it was totally conquered.

The Baptism in the Spirit

Over the next few years, however, Wigglesworth realized there was still more for him in God. Holiness was vital, but God had promised power. Acts 1:8 kept returning to his mind, the passage where Jesus promised the disciples power *after* the Holy Spirit came upon them: "But ye shall receive power, after that the Holy Ghost is come upon you. . . ."

Then he heard that the Holy Spirit had fallen upon people at All Saints Church, Sunderland. This was the spreading wave of Pentecostalism that followed the 1907 Azusa Street, California, revival. He attended the meetings, and here is the story in his own words, as he related it to John Carter:

> When this Pentecostal outpouring began in England, I went to Sunderland. I was as certain as possible that I had (already) received the Holy Spirit and was absolutely rigid in this conviction. I met with people who had assembled for the purpose of receiving the Holy Spirit, and I was continually in those meetings causing disturbances, until the people wished I had never come. But I was hungry and thirsty for God and had gone to Sunderland because I had heard that God was pouring out His Spirit in a new way, and that God had visited His people and manifested His power, and that people were speaking in tongues as on the Day of Pentecost.
>
> When I got there I said, "I cannot understand this meeting. I have left a meeting in Bradford all on fire for God. The fire fell last night, and we were all laid out under the power of God. I have come here for tongues, and I don't hear them."
>
> "Oh," they said, "when you get baptized in the Holy Spirit, you will speak in tongues."
>
> "Oh, that's it," said I, "When the presence of God came upon me, my tongue was loosed. When I went into the open air to preach, I felt I had a new tongue."

"No," they replied, "that's not it."

"What is it then?" I asked.

They said, "You'll know when you're baptized with the Holy Spirit."

"I am baptized," I interjected, "and there's no one here that can persuade me that I'm not baptized."

So I was up against them, and they were up against me. I remember a man saying, "I'd been here three weeks, then the Lord baptized me with the Holy Spirit, and I began to speak with tongues."

"Let's hear it," I said, "that's what I'm here for." But he would not talk in tongues.

As the days passed, I became more and more hungry. I had opposed the meetings so much, but the Lord was gracious. I shall ever remember the last day, the day I had to leave for home. God was with me so much as I went to the last meeting. But I could not rest. I went to the vicarage, and there in the library, I said to the vicar's wife, Mrs. Boddy, "I can rest no longer. I must have these tongues."

She said, "It is not tongues. It is the baptism you need. If you will allow God to baptize you, the other will be all right."

"My dear sister," I said, "I know I am baptized. You know I have to leave shortly. Please lay your hands on me that I may receive tongues."

She rose up and laid her hands on me, and the fire fell. (Just then) she had to go out to answer a knock on the door. It was the best thing that could have happened. I was alone with God. Then He gave me a revelation. Oh, it was wonderful!

He showed me an empty cross and Jesus glorified. Then I saw that the Lord had purified me. It seemed that God gave me a new vision, and I saw a perfect being within me with mouth open, saying, "Clean, clean, clean." When I began to repeat it, I found myself speaking with other tongues. The joy was so great, I could not utter it in my own tongue, and I worshipped God in other tongues as the Spirit gave utterance. It was all as beautiful, as peaceful, as when

Jesus said, "Peace, be still" (Mark 4:39). The tranquility of that moment and the joy surpassed anything I had ever known.

What had I received? I had received the Bible evidence.

This was Wigglesworth's real baptism in the Holy Spirit that allowed him to become the man and minister that he was in later years. He constantly urged others to seek a similar experience for themselves, then to move on into a life of continuous receiving of more and more of the blessed Spirit of God.

However, both Smith and Polly recognized that the evidence of the baptism was *more* than tongues. A prayer language was the initial evidence, but Jesus had promised power. Polly showed her perception of this when — in response to his testimony about having received the baptism in the same way as the apostles — she said, "If you've got what they had, you can do what they did."

Wigglesworth, for his part, began to pray, "Lord, show me what you baptized me for."

One day, when he was still working as a plumber, he returned to his home to find an old man had been brought there who was in need of ministry. The man was crying out that he had committed the unpardonable sin.

Immediately, Wigglesworth heard the Lord say in his heart, "This is what I baptized you for."

With this confidence in his spirit, he went into the room where the old man lay, still crying, "I'm lost, lost! I've committed the unpardonable sin."

Wigglesworth went up to him, and in the name of Jesus commanded the tormenting, lying spirit to come out of the man. Immediately, the old man was delivered, and his peace and assurance returned. And Wigglesworth heard the echo in his heart, "This is what I baptized you for."

He was not content with the *blessing* of Pentecost, he wanted to know the *power* of Pentecost. Many years after his baptism, he was taken to a resort in New Zealand for a rest after a great campaign. One evening his host asked him the secret of his power and success.

In a broken voice, and with tears slowly trickling down his face, he replied:

> I am sorry you asked me that question, but I will answer it.
>
> I am a broken-hearted man. My wife, who meant everything to me, died eleven years ago (in 1913). After the funeral, I went back and lay on her grave. I wanted to die there. But God spoke to me and told me to rise up and come away. I told him if he would give me a double portion of the Spirit — my wife's and my own — I would go and preach the Gospel.
>
> God was gracious to me and answered my request. But I sail the high seas alone. I am a lonely man, and many a time all I can do is to weep and weep.

Here was a secret indeed.

> The sacrifices of God are a broken spirit: a broken and contrite heart, O God, thou wilt not despise.
>
> Psalm 51:17

In this context, the full blessing of Pentecost was to him a costly enduement. If he went farther than others in seeking its outworking "in demonstration and power," it was because he did not want to have paid the price in vain.

For himself and others, he was utterly discontented with a baptism that did not fundamentally change a person and impart a power that had not been present before. Perhaps today we have seen too many "easy baptisms," baptisms lacking life-changing force.

Wigglesworth prayed for and received a real baptism and went on to prove and demonstrate its mighty effects.

In one city, a man invited him to his home in order to be prayed for to receive the baptism. Wigglesworth arrived to find a beautiful meal had been prepared for him. The man and his wife suggested they eat first and pray afterwards.

Wigglesworth bluntly asked, "What do you want most, a stomach full of food or a soul full of God?"

The man was shocked into the realization of his wrong priorities. Wigglesworth immediately began to share the Scripture, showed the man the need of cleansing and faith, then prayed for him. In no time at all, he was filled with the Spirit. The glory of the Lord filled the room, and the couple and Wigglesworth rejoiced together. The meal, so kindly prepared, was forgotten.

Wigglesworth's son-in-law, James Salter, later a powerful and outstanding missionary to Central Africa, told on one occasion of his experience of the need of cleansing as a prerequisite for the full baptism in the Holy Spirit. When he was in prayer, seeking the fullness of the Spirit, it seemed there was only one thing he could think about — carrots.

The more he tried to pray, the louder "carrots" echoed in his mind. He realized that God was speaking to him about something that had to be dealt with. He rose up out of the prayer meeting and went to a green grocer's shop (in America, what would be called a produce or vegetable shop) kept by a friend's father.

He waited until the shop was clear of other customers, then the shopkeeper said, "Well, Jim, lad, what do you want?"

Salter told him that often when he had stopped by the shop to see his friend, he had stolen a carrot. He had come to confess and make restitution.

"Jim, lad, we all take a carrot from time to time. It doesn't bother me," the man said.

Salter replied, "But God is bothering me about it. I must put it right."

He did, then went to the prayer meeting, sought the Lord and, in a very short time, was filled with the Holy Spirit.

Chapter 11:

Standing on Holy Ground

*W*igglesworth was the purest man I have ever known, a man who lived daily in the immediate presence of God.

Here are two illustrations:

• At one time Wigglesworth was ministering at Zion City, Illinois, founded by John Alexander Dowie. There, he called the ministers to a special prayer meeting and was already praying when they arrived. As he continued in prayer, sometimes in English and sometimes in tongues, the awesome presence of God filled the room.

One by one, the ministers were smitten by the power of God and fell prostrate on their faces. The reality of God's presence so gripped them that they were unable to move for at least an hour. Wigglesworth was the only one who remained standing as he continued in praise and prayer. A cloud, like a radiant mist, filled the room where the ministers were.

• In 1922, Wigglesworth was in Wellington, the capital city of New Zealand. One afternoon at a special meeting, eleven prominent Christians gathered for prayer at Wigglesworth's request. One after the other they prayed, until all had taken part except the visiting evangelist. He then began to pray for their city and country, and as he continued, the sense of God's presence and power so filled the room that one by one the others left, unable to continue in the blazing light of God's holiness.

One minister, hearing of this from one who had been there, greatly desired to be in a similar meeting — but with the determination that whoever else left, he would not. An opportunity soon came for him to attend such a meeting. Several people prayed, then Wigglesworth began to pray.

As he lifted up his voice, it seemed that God Himself invaded the place. Those present became deeply conscious that they were on holy ground. The power of God in its purity was like a heavy weight pressing on them. One by one, the people left until only the man remained who had set himself to stay.

He hung on and hung on until at last the pressure became a compulsion, and he could stay no longer. His own testimony was that with the floodgates of his soul pouring out a stream of tears and with uncontrollable sobbing, he had to get out of the Presence or die. He added that Wigglesworth, a man who knew God as few men do, was left alone in an atmosphere in which few men could breathe.[1]

This closeness to God, seeing what God was doing and hearing what God was saying, then doing and saying the same on earth, is clearly seen in an incident related by William Davies when pastoring in Chesterfield, Derbyshire, England.

---

[1]Roberts, Harry V. *New Zealand's Greatest Revival*. (Auckland: Pelorus Press Ltd., 1951).

Wigglesworth was conducting a crusade for Davies. One night in the healing line, there was a young man with a bandage around his throat.

When the evangelist asked him, "What's up?" he replied in a hoarse whisper, "Can God do anything for me?"

"Of course He can," answered Wigglesworth, "unless He has forgotten how to make voice boxes."

He placed his hands on the young man's throat, prayed in his usual way, then turned the young man around, saying, "Go home and eat a meal of meat and potatoes."

The young man turned back, saying, "I can't, Sir! I feed myself through this," pointing to a tube in the side of his throat.

Wigglesworth turned him around again, gave him a gentle push, and said, "Go on your way. Do as you're told. Be not faithless, but believing."

The next night, the young man was again in the healing line. When he came forward, Wigglesworth said, "What are you doing here? I prayed for you last night!"

The young man answered in a normal voice, "I've come to tell you what God did for me last night."

Turning him to face the audience, Wigglesworth said, "You don't need to tell me. Tell them," and this was the young man's testimony:

"After receiving the preacher's stern rebuke (to do as he was told), I went home and asked my mother to cook me a solid meal. She argued with me, but I told her to please prepare it. I *was* going to eat it. She prepared the meal. I sat down and took the first mouthful, chewing it a long time, hesitating to swallow it. Finally with fear and trembling, I swallowed that first mouthful. It just slipped down my throat, no pain, no obstruction, no trouble at all. Since then, I've had more meals, and I'm looking forward to one after this meeting."

Wigglesworth asked, "Then what are you doing with that bandage around your throat?"

The young fellow explained that it covered the tube through which he had been receiving food and that he was going to the hospital the next day to have it removed.

The evangelist quietly but confidently said, "What the Lord has begun, He can complete." Calling Pastor Davies and other helpers to come near, he said, "Now watch this, for you will never see the like of it again."

He removed the bandage, gently drew the tube out of the young man's neck, then placed his thumb and forefinger each side of the hole. Those who were watching were astonished. Before their very eyes, the hole healed right up. What he had seen God do in heaven, he had done on earth.

He often said, "What I have, you can have." And we can! but there is the same price to pay. We must be holy. We must live very close to Jesus. We must dwell in the presence of God.

Beyond contradiction, Wigglesworth's emphasis on holiness was a major factor in the amazing results of his ministry. There was a sense of awe in his meetings. One businessman had his unsaved secretary attend those Wellington meetings to record what was said and what took place. Later, this was his testimony:

> During the address, the evangelist suddenly burst into tongues and then gave an interpretation. I said to my typist, "Take that down," and a few moments later, "Did you get that down?" She said, "I'm sorry, but everything went strange, and I couldn't lift my hand." A little later, another message was given, and I again made request, but the pencil had fallen from her hand, and she was trembling

like an aspen leaf. At the end of the meeting, she responded to the evangelist's plea and accepted Christ as her Savior.[2]

[2]New Zealand's Greatest Revival, p. 11.

Chapter 12:

To Hunger and Thirst After Righteousness

*M*oses Copeland, a British preacher, said that in his youth he was given this word by Smith Wigglesworth: "When the child of God ceases to hunger after righteousness and purity, then Satan gets in."

His own way of preventing so sad a development was to nourish his life by communion with God. Once he had heard a godly minister tell this story:

> There was a time in my life when I sensed that God was calling me to come apart and seek his face. But I was busy, and I would go on with those things that were keeping me busy. God was gracious and persisted in calling me. Bit by bit, I began to respond, until I formed the habit of going aside at the slightest breath of the Spirit to spend time with God.

This impressed Wigglesworth, and he developed the same habit. At home with his family or even in other people's homes, if he sensed a prompting in his spirit, he would quietly withdraw from company, go to his room, and enjoy the Lord's presence.

Leslie, his grandson, told me that his grandfather would pray a while, then lie on the bed and open his Bible "to see what Father had to say." Then he would meditate and worship, often in other tongues. Then he would pray again and repeat the process, until sometimes several hours would pass. He was following the advice of the psalmist David: "When thou saidst, Seek ye my face; my heart said with thee, Thy face, Lord, will I seek" (Ps. 27:8).

In his earlier years, he prayed for long periods. At times, he spent whole nights in prayer for souls. He told me in later years, "These days (when he was traveling long hours, staying in different homes, and holding meetings all over the world) I cannot pray for half an hour on end. But there is not a half-hour of my waking life that I am not in prayer some time."

Everything he did was bathed in that communion with God — conversation, letter writing, preparing for ministry, preaching, or bringing healing and deliverance to multitudes. His chairmanship of meetings was likewise saturated with God.

For long years one of the largest Pentecostal conventions in England was at Preston, Lancashire — the Easter Convention I have referred to earlier in this book. The convention was four days long with three meetings scheduled each day. The local pastor, Dick Coates, was a precious brother but not gifted in leading large meetings.

He and the elders invited Wigglesworth to be chairman. And what a chairman! He imparted something of the Spirit from the moment he entered the building. Few people knew, however, that every year before the convention he went away for a week to a quiet place to seek God's face for His anointing on every meeting, every preacher, every song.

The consequence was that every meeting he conducted was in the Spirit from the opening moment. No almost endless singing of choruses to get the people in the "right mood" and no tiring standing for long periods so that the congregation was too weary to appreciate the ministry of the Word.

Often the first speaker was up and preaching ten minutes after the service began, preaching to a Spirit-quickened, fresh, and responsive audience. Often, after the first song, Wigglesworth would ask the congregation, "Who wants a blessing? Put one hand up." The congregation would respond. Then, "Who wants a double blessing? Put two hands up." Again, there would be a response. Finally, he would say, "If you want a blessing you can take home with you, everyone stand up. Now, pray out loud." There were congregations up to two thousand, and when they obeyed Wigglesworth's instructions, it was like the sound of many waters, and the glory of God filled the place.

A friend who had been a "high churchman" told me of being at one of the conventions and being so horrified at what he thought was irreverence that he left the building.

He had not gone far when God spoke to him, "If you don't go back and enter into that prayer and praise, I will cease to bless you."

He hurried back and entered into the worship as God had commanded. His testimony to me was that the worship time at the convention became a powerful force for change in his life. And it flowed out of Wigglesworth's communion with God.

That communion was nourished by partaking of holy communion. He did this every day whether he was at home or not. If other believers were with him, he would share with them. If not, he would partake alone.

He kept from spiritual stagnation by eagerly pursuing the Lord. Following is his own testimony to the various ways he was led as he followed on to know the Lord. All of those ways meant some measure of upheaval in his life, but he felt no price was too high to pay to live in ever-deepening communion with God.

When I was in the Methodist Church, I was sure I was saved and sure I was right. The Lord said to me, "Come out," and I came out. When I was with the people known as the Brethren, I was sure that *now* I was right. But the Lord said, "Come out," and I went into the Salvation Army. At that time (the founding days of the Army), it was full of life, and there were revivals everywhere; but the Salvation Army went into natural things, and the great revivals I had known in the early days ceased. The Lord said to me, "Come out," and I came out. I have had to "come out" three times since.

I believe this Pentecostal revival we are now in is the best thing the Lord has on earth today. Yet I believe that out of this, the Lord has something still better. God has no use for any man who is not hungering and thirsting for yet more of Himself and His righteousness. The Lord has told us to covet earnestly the best gifts, and we need to be covetous for those that will bring the most glory to God.

His eager pursuit after God led to an unbroken sense of the presence of God. He would tell us, "You have to live ready. If you have to stop to get ready, you are too late. The opportunity will have gone."

A good illustration of this is the time a sick man asked me to bring Wigglesworth to his home to pray for him. I did, and introduced them to each other.

After only a few minutes, Wigglesworth said, "God has told me not to pray for you till you repent of your sin, your backsliding, your pride, and your unbelief."

The man said, "I don't know what you are talking about."

Wigglesworth said, "You do. The Holy Spirit is not a liar."

The man's wife pleaded with him, but he told her to keep out of it.

Wigglesworth prayed, "Lord, give this man repentance," and walked out. When we were outside, he began to weep and said, "Why did I have to say that?"

I told him the man had been a deacon in our church, but he had left us and joined a liberal church where he was publishing literature against the baptism in the Spirit.

"Then why did you take me there?" he asked.

I replied, "Because he asked me, and I felt a fresh voice might help him back to God."

The next day, Wigglesworth sent me to see if the man was ready to be prayed for, but his wife greeted me at the door saying, "I don't think you had better see my husband today. He's still angry at Wigglesworth and you."

I said, "I'd rather see your husband than go back and tell Smith Wigglesworth that I didn't see him!"

When I entered the sick room, the man said, "You don't agree with Wigglesworth, do you?"

I replied, "I know, and you know, that what he said is true, but I didn't have the courage to say it to you before."

"Get out, and don't come back!" he shouted. That was the last I saw of him. He died shortly afterwards. But that incident showed me that Wigglesworth was always ready to hear God and follow his instructions.

The Importance of Praise

It would be a serious omission if I did not tell of the importance of praise in Wigglesworth's life. A. L. Hoy, shortly after he was saved, had tea with Wigglesworth and asked him what he thought pleased God most.

Wigglesworth looked at him, his eyes shining, and instantly replied, "Worship! No man enjoys more the riches of divine grace and performs the Lord's will to a higher degree than the man who walks with God in continuous worship."[1]

He had unique ways of bringing home this truth. Once as he came to the platform before a large congregation, he said, "How many of you came in properly tonight? I mean with both hands in the air, praising the Lord."

No one raised a hand.

He then said, "Go out, the lot of you, and come in properly. The Scripture says 'Enter into his gates with thanksgiving, and into his courts with praise' (Ps. 100:4)."

Out they all went and came back joyfully praising the Lord. They had a most wonderful meeting. More than forty years later, I told this story in one church, and a lady came up excitedly to say that she had been in that meeting and that it happened just as I had reported it.

At Lullingstone, Kent, England, there is the excavation of a Roman villa, the foundation of which was laid A.D. 90. As the work proceeded, they found a chapel, and on the wall of the chapel, a plaster painting. It depicted a man and woman standing with hands in the air obviously singing. The work dates back to 320 A.D., and the archaeologist gave it the title, "Early Christians at Worship." From earliest times, Spirit-filled people have been a praising people.

---

[1] *Elim Evangel* 3.676.

Ministering the Spirit

One of his joys in his experience of the consciousness of God's presence was that it enabled him to "minister the Holy Spirit." On more than one occasion, he said to me, "If you don't minister the Holy Spirit, you minister death."

When Jack West was a young Canadian evangelist, he called to see Brother Wigglesworth at his home in Bradford, Yorkshire, England. Wigglesworth was away, but Jack was invited to stay overnight. He slept in the evangelist's bed and declared, "I verily felt the power of God in that bedroom."

The next day, Wigglesworth arrived home and prayed for West, "Lord, don't let this man be ordinary. Make him extraordinary." Jack said that he remained under the power of God for many days and began a ministry that God confirmed "with signs following" because God's servant had "ministered the Holy Spirit."

Pastor George Miles, who lived for many years only a short distance from Wigglesworth, often visited him. This is his witness:

"Mr. Wigglesworth was so filled with God that his little home in Bradford seemed to be holy ground, and like Moses of old, I wanted to remove the shoes from my feet in an act of reverence."

The best way I can clarify what he meant by "ministering the Spirit" is to say that he "believed into" what he spoke, whether in conversation, preaching, prayer, or prophecy. With him, there were no idle words. He, by faith, actively associated the Holy Spirit with his ministry. He believed God was with him, was anointing what he was saying and doing, even as he was in the act of ministering. His faith communicated this fact to many of his hearers.

In one church, he said, "I'll go out, and come back in. Everyone who touches me will be healed." Sad to say, only one woman touched him, but she was healed.

Wigglesworth believed it was possible, and often necessary, to begin in the natural and by faith rise to the spiritual. His total acceptance of the verse in Second Timothy that talks of "stirring up the gift in you" (2 Tim. 1:6) led to his sometimes criticized statement, "If the Holy Spirit doesn't move me, I move the Holy Spirit."

Anyone with the slightest knowledge of Smith Wigglesworth could never imagine there was the least bit of flippancy or irreverence in that remark. His deep sense of the awesomeness of God's presence would preclude that. But he knew there were times when, without a conscious awareness of being moved by God, he had to step out in faith. He knew that as he moved towards God in faith, God would move toward him in power. In this sense only, would he say that he "moved" the Holy Spirit.

Chapter 13:

His First Desire Was Witnessing

*S*mith Wigglesworth's primary goal in ministry was soulwinning, and winning souls was not a "program" he felt was his duty to carry out, nor did soulwinning become "works." The best way to describe his success in getting people born again is that soulwinning was the spontaneous result of his relationship with the Lord.

In a sense, he no more tried to get people saved than an apple tree "tries" to grow apples or a vine "tries" to produce grapes. He truly was grafted into Christ, and his branch was abiding. (John 15.) His leaves were open to heaven. He made sure of the daily, continuous flow of the sap — the life of the Spirit.

For him, there was a "cycle of the life in the Holy Spirit," and he lived in that cycle.

A second aspect of his soulwinning ability is the baptism in the Spirit. From the day of his conversion, he was a soulwinner. In fact, the first person he got saved was his mother — and later he led his father to the Lord! But he was much more a soulwinner after he was baptized in the Holy Spirit. The baptism gave him a keen sense of the value of a soul.

He was saddened by those who enjoyed the baptism for the pleasure it gave them and did not press on to its primary purpose as declared by Jesus in Acts 1:8: "Ye shall receive power after that the Holy Ghost is come upon you: and ye shall be *witnesses* unto me."

He once said:

> Now, beloved, I am out for men. It is my business to be out for men. It is my business to make everybody hungry, dissatisfied. It is my business to make people either glad or mad. I have a message from heaven that will not leave people as I find them.[1]

When he stayed in our home in England, we lived in a lovely resort, Leigh-on-Sea. From pleasant gardens on the Marine Parade ("boardwalk" in America), you could look over the broad estuary of the River Thames to Kent. From the Marine Parade, one hundred and fifty steps led down to the railway station. People who came home by train had to climb those steps.

At the top of the steps was a bench, and day after day Wigglesworth would sit there enjoying the sun. He would take out his New Testament to "see what Father has to say." Then he would meditate and pray. But always he was alert for opportunities to reach people for God.

In the spirit of what he felt was his "business" not to leave people as he found them, he would speak to people passing the bench on which he was sitting.

As he saw older people struggling up the last of those steps, he would bluntly ask, "Are you ready to die?"

---

[1] *Faith That Prevails*, p. 51.

A shock approach indeed — and hardly "textbook evangelism"! Yet so real was his concern and so deep his compassion that few took offense. Such an anointing rested on him that several were won for the Lord.

One young couple approached him climbing the steps and walking as far apart on the six-foot-wide steps as they could get.

He called them to him and asked in a kindly voice, "What's wrong? Quarreled?"

Indeed they had and decided that their marriage was finished. He invited them to sit, one on each side of him, and with a fatherly arm around each, he led them to Jesus. Arm in arm, and with shining eyes, they went on their way, their souls saved, and their marriage healed.

His passion for souls began when he was saved and lasted all of his life. As a boy, he frequently witnessed to his school fellows, not always wisely or tactfully, but always earnestly.

When he was in the Salvation Army, he would spend Saturday nights in prayer claiming fifty to a hundred souls each week. When he told of this later, he would add, "and we knew that we would get them." He could not understand what he called "modern indifference to soulwinning and modern-day occupation with trivialities."

For a time before his marriage, he lived in Liverpool, England, and at the weekend, he gathered together poor children. He spent his wages to provide their physical needs as far as he could, then told them about Jesus. There was never a Sunday during that period but what at least fifty children were born again.

George Miles, whom I have mentioned before in this book, tells of an interesting and challenging situation. Here it is in his own words:

Many years ago, after an American visitor had ministered in our Bridge Street Church, it was my privilege, on the Monday following, to escort the preacher to the home of that great man of God, Smith Wigglesworth. I shall never forget that visit and the deep impression it made on my life when I was but a young (assistant) pastor longing for the deeper things of God. Mr. Wigglesworth was so filled with God that his little home in Bradford seemed to be holy ground, and like Moses of old, I wanted to remove the shoes from my feet in an act of reverence.

Five times during our short stay in the Victor Road house, Mr. Wigglesworth interrupted the conversation, taking a well-worn New Testament from his pocket, saying, "Now, Brethren, let us pause a moment to hear what Father has to say." (Each time) he read a few verses, gave a brief exhortation, then offered an earnest prayer which made us realized we were very near to God.

Afterwards, as I reflected on those precious moments of communion, I felt this must be what the Apostle Paul meant when he spoke of "living in the Spirit," or what our Lord inferred when He made mention of His Word abiding in us. I was profoundly aware that God was in that place. Even during dinner, we heard again "what Father has to say."

When the meal came to an end, Mr. Wigglesworth looked at me and said, "Young man, have you got any petrol (gasoline) in your car?" The query about petrol was understandable; we were living in World War II days, and it was strictly rationed for essential purposes. When Mr. Wigglesworth discovered I had a supply of petrol, he said, "Good, we will go for a short outing." I felt a few qualms about using petrol for this purpose, but the man of God seemed to be so completely in control that I felt nothing could go wrong under such authority.

Mr. Wigglesworth asked our visitor to sit in the rear of the car, while he himself would sit next to the driver to direct the way. I remember it all so vividly. As soon as Mr. Wigglesworth got in the car, he lifted his hands heavenward and prayed so earnestly — and yet so naturally — "Lord, bless this young man. Bless this car," and then he added, "Lord, bless these tires."

Now, I must explain. I said a fervent "amen" to this last request, for in those days, we were compelled to use synthetic car tires, and quite unknown to Mr. Wigglesworth, there was a nasty gaping split in one of my rear tires through which the inner tube was clearly visible. What a good thing it was that the man of faith included the tires in his report!

After traveling for some distance, we arrived at the foot of Ilkley Moor, a Yorkshire beauty spot. Immediately before us was a narrow, unpaved flinty road leading up the moor.

To my astonishment, my guide said, "Ah, yes. This is the road we want. Go straight ahead, young man." My heart sank.

I thought, "I'll never get up here without a puncture." But we did, you know. What would have happened had not Mr. Wigglesworth prayed, "Lord, bless these tires"?

Arriving safely on the top of the moors on that lovely June day, we sat for a while on a convenient seat while that remarkable man captivated us with some of his amazing experiences. Then the American preacher and I went for a short stroll on those glorious hills, leaving Mr. Wigglesworth to enjoy a few quiet minutes basking in the sunshine.

When we returned, we found our brother and another man kneeling at the bench, both of them engrossed in fervent prayer.

As we stood waiting for the prayers to finish, I sensed again the sacred atmosphere which I had breathed in his home. As the two men got up from their knees, Mr. Wigglesworth introduced us to the stranger with whom he had been praying.

He said to me, "Now, young man, this brother has to go into the hospital tomorrow for a major operation. He used to be a servant of God, but had backslidden and got right away from the Savior. But today, he has come back home to God and now, whatever happens in the hospital, his soul is right with God."

The man, with a radiant face, happy in God's restoring grace, gladly gave testimony to what the Lord had done for him. Then Mr. Wigglesworth said, "I knew I had to come up here today. Father sent me. Now our task is fulfilled, we will give glory to God as we return home."

I drove my car all the way down that flinty road back to Bradford, then home to Leeds. The inner tube was still to be seen through the split in my tire, but I never had any trouble. Furthermore, I felt quite sure the precious rationed petrol had been used for an essential purpose.

Right through to old age, Wigglesworth sought the lost. There was a park near his home, and few people who frequented it were missed in his witnessing. He shared Christ with almost all he met, whether walking or riding.

Chapter 14:

Six Ways He Reached the Lost

*L*et me share with you some of the ways Wigglesworth sought and won the lost. They are *personal evangelism*, some illustrations of which have already been given; inquiry room work; open-air preaching (in America, this is called "street preaching"); house-to-house visitation; evangelistic preaching, and missions.

Another example of his always-ready personal evangelism concerns a railway journey he once made and later told me about. When the train stopped at one station, two ladies boarded it.

He saw the worried look on their faces and said bluntly, but compassionately, "You look miserable, what's wrong?"

They told him one of them was going into the hospital to have her leg amputated. He spoke to them about Jesus and tenderly led them to the Savior. Then he went on to show them that the One Who saves also is able to heal. He prayed for the sick woman, and her leg was healed. When she arrived at the hospital, doctors could find nothing wrong with it.

In 1985, I was preaching in Edmonton, Alberta, Canada. A retired pastor came to tell me there had been a lady in the church he formerly pastored who, as a teenager, had worked as a servant in a home where Wigglesworth was entertained. The employer of this girl had introduced her to his distinguished guest.

Her first name was "Grace," and Wigglesworth immediately said, "Oh, I found your name in the Bible."

Then he read Ephesians 2:8 to her: "By grace are ye saved through faith; and that not of yourselves: it is the gift of God." And he led her to Jesus.

That pastor declared that although the girl had been brought to Jesus in such a simple, almost simplistic, way, she was for fifty years afterwards one of the finest members of his church.

One day, God spoke to Wigglesworth telling him to go to a certain spot by the side of a street in Bradford and wait for a man he would send. He went and waited half an hour, then he waited an hour. After waiting an hour and a half, he was on the point of leaving when he saw approaching him a man driving a horse and carriage.

"This is the man," prompted the Holy Spirit.

Wigglesworth jumped up and sat on the seat by the side of the driver. He was ordered off but stayed put. Lovingly, earnestly, patiently, God's servant spoke to the driver about his need of Jesus. Before they arrived at his destination, the man yielded to the Savior's claim. Very shortly after that, news came that the man suddenly had been taken ill and died, and with the news came a message that he had died trusting in the Lord.

God can so use all of us. One day in England, I was driving past a gypsy encampment. Only the day before, I had visited a fine Christian gypsy named Ken there. But I felt a strong urge to stop and visit him again. I got out of my car and began to walk across the field toward the shack he called home. Coming toward me was Ken's brother, Gilbert.

He looked at me in astonishment, saying, "Thank God, you've come."

"Why?" I asked.

"The old man (their father) is dying, and he's calling for you," Ken said.

I went into a lean-to attached to Ken's shack and found "Old Man" Buckley, as he was called, very sick. He was lying on old clothes and blankets on a dirt floor. He had been a wicked man. Every one of his sons had been in jail, and he had avoided jail only by his cunning.

I knelt by the side of his "bed," and said, "Mr. Buckley, I'm here. What can I do for you?"

"Oh, Pastor," he said, "I want to find God, and I don't know how."

It was a joy to point him to Jesus. A few days later, he died.

Ken, the Christian son, told me, "The old man had been such a wicked sinner I had always been afraid he would have a dreadful death. But Jesus saved him, and he had a peaceful end. He died happy in Jesus. Wonderful Jesus!"

Wigglesworth knew the excitement of great crusade meetings where he saw thousands come to the altar for salvation. But he never lost sight of the value of one soul. To the very last day of his life, he sought to win souls.

Inquiry Room Work

Today, the "inquiry room" is called the "counseling room." The earlier name for the room meant something, however. People were not just there to discuss their problems. They were there to "inquire" how their sins could be forgiven.

In the earlier days of Wigglesworth's soulwinning work, both in the Salvation Army and at the Bowland Street Mission, his wife was the preacher. He worked at the altar or in the inquiry room.

He used to say, "Polly put down the net. I landed the fish."

He wanted to make as sure as possible that the inquirers received a real salvation. He believed that strong births make healthy babies.

All Christians can, and should, prepare so that they are able to lead people to Jesus. My own soulwinning ministry began effectively in 1930 when, in a time of revival, souls were being won to Christ in my home church in Birmingham, England. But like many Christians, I began in embarrassment.

My pastor asked me to take charge of the inquiry room work. Ten to twenty people were responding to the gospel in every service, seven nights a week. They needed direction. I had to decline, because even though I had been saved many years, I did not know how to lead anyone to saving faith in Jesus.

This so convicted me that I went home determined to learn how to answer any inquiry about the Lord. I studied the Word and soulwinning books and prayed. After a month, I went back and asked my pastor if the job was still open. Happily for me, it was, and for some years — until I moved into full-time ministry — I had the joyous privilege of dealing with hundreds of souls in crisis.

Open-Air Preaching

This kind of preaching is not so much in style today in our modern civilization, but in Wigglesworth's time, it was a major way of effectively reaching out with the gospel. He used it extensively because he believed in getting out where the sinners were.

He was never a polished preacher. His homiletics were non-existent, but his dynamics were mighty! His deep love for Jesus, his passion for souls, and his earnestness secured an entrance for his message. He won many souls who confessed Christ publicly through this kind of ministry.

His son-in-law wrote after his death, "He grew in grace and zeal for God, and his highest happiness was found in pointing others to the Lord Jesus. He tramped the country roads with that one purpose . . . To his dying day, he lived for this one thing, rarely coming home — morning, afternoon, or night — but what he had led someone to the Lord or ministered healing to a needy person."

House-to-House Visitation

Before visiting door to door was popular in England, Wigglesworth did it. He did not wait for his church to develop a visitation program. He *was* the program! With burning heart and unflagging zeal, he sought out people in their homes. He had what has been called "20/20 spiritual vision" — Acts 20:20.

Always he prepared for this visitation evangelism with much prayer. Although he witnessed freely, he did not witness indiscriminately, which is a very important point! *He waited on God for direction as well as power.* An example of this occurred when he stayed at Roker in Sunderland with Pastor Fred Johnson.

There was an elevator to the beach, and some men were working on it. At their invitation, he rode down with them and back up. Pastor Johnson remained at the top, but he was sure Wigglesworth would witness to the men.

When he returned, Johnson asked, "Did you give them a word?"

And Wigglesworth replied, "No, I wasn't to pray for them. I wasn't to do anything at all. I was one with them in a way. But I left something behind for them — that was the presence of God. It was more real than a tract."

Because he carried this "sweet savor" of Christ and was so compassionate and earnest, Wigglesworth rarely was refused admission to the homes at which he called. He prayed in every home, and in so many, he did vital work for Jesus. Eternity alone will reveal how many were born again at their own firesides or in their own kitchens though the dedicated visitation ministry of God's servant, Smith Wigglesworth.

Evangelistic Preaching

When he joined the Salvation Army as a young man, the young lady who later became his beloved Polly was the lieutenant in charge of the local corps, and in the beginning of their marriage, she did the preaching. After his return from Sunderland, claiming to have received the baptism in the Spirit "as on the Day of Pentecost," Polly insisted that he preach.

Previously, he had not been able to say more than a few words before breaking down weeping, but this time, he preached with fire and a torrent of words. All Polly could do was say, "That's not *my* Smith! That's not *my* Smith! What's happened to the man?"

From that day on, he preached without training, but he never preached without fire. God was able to love people through Smith Wigglesworth. With that love pouring through him, and the powerful anointing of God's Spirit resting on him, he made Christ fully known to his hearers.

He preached in Bowland Street Mission, in churches all over the world, in factories, quarries, and in tents. He preached in his homeland and around the world. While most seem to remember him for his ministry of the miraculous, his greatest ministry was in the winning of the lost. Here are some of his comments in New Zealand in the 1922 series of meetings:

"Healing of the body is not the main thing."

"I would sooner have one soul saved than ten thousand healed."

"I preach and practice healing to attract people just as our Lord did."

"My main aim is to win men for Christ."

Multiplied thousands came to a saving knowledge of Jesus as Lord under his ministry. In Ceylon, sometimes thousands of people at a time cried to God for salvation. In Norway, on one occasion, when the Town Hall was full and hundreds were outside unable to get in, the Lord spoke to him as he preached, and said, "If you ask Me, I will give you every soul in this place."

For a moment, he hesitated, then asked. He told later with awe how the power of God swept the place, and how people cried out for mercy all over the building.

He would add, "I verily believe that God *gave* me every soul."

In South Africa, so great were the evangelistic results of his ministry that the results reached far beyond his meetings. Justus du Plessis, his interpreter there, whom I have mentioned before, gave his considered opinion that the whole of the country was affected. It was the same everywhere, even when he traveled on shipboard.

The story of his "concert" on one ship has often been told, but here it is in his own words as told to John Carter, who gave it to me just as it was given to him:

When the ship began to move, I said to the people, "I'm going to preach on this ship on Sunday. Will you come and hear me?"

"No," they said. Later they came around and said, "We're going to have an entertainment, and we would like you to be in it."

I said, "Come back in a quarter of an hour."

They came around again and said, "Are you ready?"

"Yes," I told them.

"What can you do?"

"I can sing," was my reply. They asked what position I wanted on the program, and I asked what would be on the program.

They said, "Songs, recitations, instrument(als), many things."

"What do you finish up with?" I asked.

"A dance."

Then I said, "Put me down just before the dance."

I went to the entertainment, and when I saw the people, it turned me to prayer. Every hour had been bathed in prayer. When I heard all their pieces, my turn came. When I showed the pianist the music, she said she couldn't play it.

I said, "Be at peace, young lady, I have the music and words inside." So I sang, "If I could only tell Him as I know Him, my Redeemer Who has brightened all my way."

God took it up, and from the least to the greatest, they were weeping. They never had a dance, but they had a prayer meeting.

And six young men were saved by the power of God in my cabin. Every day God was saving people on that ship.

Missions

Wigglesworth was never a missionary in the literal meaning of the word, but he had a passion for overseas missions. You needed only to see him at missionary conventions to realize his enthusiasm for missions. He would lead the missionary giving, pray for the missionary candidates, encourage the missionaries on furlough, and call for volunteers. He freely gave his own daughter, Alice, to the work, first in Angola, then in South America, and later in the Congo.

His delight in the wide sales of his sermon book, *Ever Increasing Faith*, was not only in the spreading of the message God had given him, but also in the fact that the profit went entirely to missions.

When he gave a copy to his young friend, Willie Hacking, he said, "Now, Brother Hacking, don't lend this book. It's not for lending. If this book is lent, folks won't buy it, and we want them to buy it. This book has made twenty thousand pounds for missions." (At that time, that amount was about a hundred times a working man's wages for a year!)

His great zeal for missions was displayed when his grandson, Leslie Wigglesworth, sailed for the Congo from Tilbury, Essex, England, in 1934. Leslie was accompanied by Alfred Brown, Jim Fowler, and Fred and Isobel Ramsbottom and their baby, Alan. Wigglesworth went to the dock to see them off and bid them "Godspeed."

As the boat pulled away, he shouted across the widening gap, "Hallelujah!" And the young missionaries responded, "Praise the

Lord!" Smith Wigglesworth, with his remarkably clear voice, continued to shout until he could not be seen. The incident conveyed to Leslie a strong sense that the spiritual link with him and a godly grandfather was unbroken.

Said one of the others, "It imparted spiritual life to a group of young missionaries."

When on crusades, he would sometimes ask that in place of a love offering for himself, a missionary offering should be taken.

"Also," he said on one occasion, "today many are not laying themselves out for soulwinning but for fleshly manifestations."

Ian MacPherson, a Scottish Pentecostal preacher, put it succinctly, "We are in danger of becoming little groups of Pentecostal specialists feeling each other's pulses."

One day in Jerusalem, Wigglesworth said to a young missionary concerning a backslider, "It's killing me, the thought of anyone turning back."

This deep sense of the lostness of people apart from Christ, this sharing of the compassion of the Savior Himself, could only come from "the love of God shed abroad in our hearts by the Holy Ghost which is given unto us" (Rom. 5:5).

As an ambassador for Christ, Wigglesworth continually besought men, "Be ye reconciled to God" (2 Cor. 5:20).

The Church today has the greatest evangelistic opportunity it ever has had. More souls are being won, and there are more souls to win than ever before in history. Let us arise to the task, inspired afresh by what God did through Smith Wigglesworth!

Chapter 15:

Wigglesworth's Healing Ministry

Wigglesworth experienced the healing power of God in his own body. Early in his ministry, he suffered greatly from hemorrhoids and used natural means for relief. His wife challenged him on preaching one thing and practicing another, and he realized he was acting inconsistently with his professed belief. He repented, looked to God, and was healed. From that day, he was committed to God as his only healer.

He had many physical trials, the greatest of which no doubt was his battle with kidney stones. He suffered much pain until, finally, at his family's urging, he went to a doctor who diagnosed his condition and said surgery was essential.

Wigglesworth thanked him and said he would trust God to do the surgery. What a test that was! He believed God would break the stones, and He did. But cleansing his system of all the broken pieces was a long and agonizing process. All of the time, he continued preaching, sometimes getting up from bed to preach and minister, then returning straight to bed.

In one service, he said, "I do not understand the ways of God! Here He is healing under my ministry, and yet, as I am preaching to you, I am suffering excruciating pains from kidney stones coming down from my body."

He never cared about "preserving his image" and was not ashamed to confess that he was suffering. There were for him mysteries about God's dealings in sickness. More than once, he declared, "Whoso can explain divine healing can explain God."

But he persisted in faith, and the final day of deliverance came. For years afterward, he carried with him a small bottle containing the broken stones God had removed.

The last time I saw him was at Bloomsbury Chapel, London, where he had been speaking. He was over eighty-six and had been so ill that his loved ones thought he had died. Yet here he was ministering again in power.

In a later letter, written to me in his own hand, he described the heart of his experience. These are his exact words and spelling:

> God is fulfilling His Word, Romans 8 ch verces 11 & 12, 13 the same Spirit that rose up Jesus from the grave quickened His mortal body as also quickened my mortal body.

Not good grammar, but good Holy Spirit reality!

His Ministry to Others

Here are some instances of healing given in his own words:

> In Sydney, Australia, a man with a stick passed a friend and me. He had to get down and twist over, and the tortures on his face made a deep impression on my soul.
>
> I asked myself, "Is it right to pass this man?"
>
> So I said to my friend, "There is a man in awful distress, and I cannot go further. I must speak to him."
>
> I went over to that man and said, "You seem in great trouble."

"Yes," he said, "I am no good, and never will be."

I said, "You see that hotel. Be in front of that door in five minutes, and I will pray for you, and you shall be as straight as any man in this place."

I came back after paying a bill, and he was there. I will never forget him wondering if he was going to be trapped, or what was up that a man should stop him in the street and tell him he was going to be straight. But I had said it, so it must be! If you say anything, you must turn with God to make it so. Never say anything for bravado, without you have the right to say it. Always be sure of your ground and that you are honoring God. Your whole ministry will have to be on the line of grace and blessing.

We helped him up the two steps and through the lobby to the elevator and took him up to my floor. It was difficult to get him from the elevator to my room as though Satan was making a last strike for his life. But we got him there. Then in five minutes this man walked out of that room as straight as any man in this place. Oh, brother, it is ministration, it is operation, it is manifestation. Those are the three leading principles of the baptism with the Holy Ghost, and we must see to it that God is producing these three through us.

Here is something different from Wigglesworth:

In a place in England, I was dealing on the lines of faith and what would take place if we believed God. Many things happened. One man, who worked in a colliery, heard me. He was in trouble with a stiff knee.

He said to his wife, "I cannot help but think every day that that message of Wigglesworth's was to stir us to do something. I cannot get away from it. All the men in the pit know that I walk with a stiff knee and how you wrap it round with yards of flannel. Well, I'm going to act. You have to be the congregation."

He got his wife in front of him, saying, "I'm going to act and do just like Wigglesworth." He got hold of his leg unmercifully, saying,

"Come out, you devils, come out!" Then he cried out, "Wife, they're gone! This is too good to keep to myself. I'm going to act now!"

He went to his place of worship, and many miners were there. It was a prayer meeting, and he told them what had happened. They were delighted. Then one said, "Jack, come over here and help me." And Jack went. As soon as he was through in one home, he was invited to another, loosing people from their many pains.

If you do it outside of Jesus, you do it for yourself; if you do it, because you want to be someone, it will be a failure. We shall only be able to do well, if we do it in the name of Jesus. Live in the Spirit, walk in the Spirit, walk in communion of the Spirit, talk with God. All the leadings of the first order are for you.

When he was in the plumbing business, he received urgent calls for prayer and sometimes could not wait to wash before he went to pray.

He said, "With my hands all black, I would preach to those sick ones with my heart aglow with love. You have to get right to the bottom of cancer with a divine compassion, and then you will see the gifts of the Spirit in operation."

He was called at 10 p.m. once to pray for a young woman dying of consumption. The doctor gave no hope at all. When Wigglesworth arrived, he saw how things were and told the mother, as well as the rest of the family, to go to bed.

When they refused, he put on his overcoat and said, "Goodbye, I'm off."

Then they changed their minds and went to bed. He knew God would move nothing in an atmosphere of unbelief and natural sympathy. He stayed.

He later said, "That was a time I surely came face to face with death and the devil."

What a fight he had, praying from 11 p.m. to 3:30 a.m. He saw her pass away.

He said, "The devil told me, 'Now you are done for. The girl has died on your hands.' "

He replied, "It can't be. God didn't send me here for nothing."

Wigglesworth knew it was time, as he put it, "to change strength." He knew that the God who could divide the Red Sea was just the same.

The devil said, "No" but Wigglesworth said, "Yes."

Here is what he said happened:

I looked at the window, and at that moment, the face of Jesus appeared. It seemed as if a million rays of light were coming from His face. He looked at the young woman who had just passed away. As He did so, the color came back into her face. She rolled over and fell asleep. Then I had a glorious time!

In the morning, the young lady woke early, put on her robe, and walked to the piano. She started to play and sing a wonderful song. Her mother and family came down to listen. The Lord had undertaken, and a miracle had occurred.

His Motivation

He ministered healing because he believed healing was God's purpose. The Word of Jesus was to Wigglesworth the final authority.

He told me personally that he often was asked for a good tract on divine healing, but would always say, "What's wrong with Matthew, Mark, Luke, and John? They are the best tracts on divine healing. They are full of cases that show the marvelous power of Jesus. They will never fail to bring God's work to pass if only people will believe them."

Another important motive for him was compassion, as I have talked about earlier in this book. I have written of how he would weep as he saw, or heard of, the desperate conditions of many of those who asked him for prayer. Sometimes his compassionate sobs were so deep that an entire congregation would weep with him.

Repeatedly in the Gospels, we are told of Jesus' compassion. Because Wigglesworth was filled with the Spirit of Christ, he, too, ministered that same Spirit. Compassion is born of love, and faith works by love. (Gal. 5:6.)

A third motivation was his passionate desire to glorify God. He was always careful to attribute every miracle of salvation, healing, or deliverance to the grace and power of God. He did not care who got the credit as long as God got the glory.

His Methods

First, he anointed with oil on the basis of Mark 6:13 and James 5:14. He had a vivid realization that the oil symbolized the Holy Spirit. As he obeyed the promise and used the symbol, he expected to see God work in healing power through the Holy Spirit.

His introduction to this method was perhaps typical. Someone pointed out to him that Scripture commands us to anoint with oil when praying for the sick. Instantly, he decided to obey God's Word. He had no idea how much oil to use, so when he was next called to pray for someone — a dying woman — he poured a whole bottle of olive oil over her. Wonderful to relate, there was granted immediately a vision of Jesus. The woman was healed.

So committed was he to anointing that he used his practical skill to develop a leak-proof bottle so that he and other preachers could have oil always on hand. In those days, we did not feel properly dressed for our job if we did not have our "Wigglesworth oil bottle" with us!

At other times, he would simply lay hands on the sick as commanded in Mark 16:18. Sometimes his laying on of hands was over-vigorous, but God honored the man's heart sincerity and faith, not the method.

He also used handkerchiefs as points of contact, having in mind Acts 19:12. Almost every mail brought handkerchiefs with requests for prayer. He always responded in faith. Following is a letter he received from Calgary, Alberta, Canada:

Dear Brother Wigglesworth:

I praise and thank the Lord Jesus Christ. It was in March 1932 that I received the handkerchief I had sent to you to anoint with oil and pray for me. I had many forms of rheumatism, arthritis, synovitis, and sciatica for twenty years from 1912-1932. I was in constant misery. During that time, I took fifty thousand aspirins besides everything the doctors could give me. Only the Lord could have kept my stomach from the effects of what I swallowed.

When I got the handkerchief from you, all my pains left that same afternoon, and all the swelling in my arms and legs was gone three days later. From that day to this, I have had no rheumatism and have not been crippled in any way. I have not taken a single aspirin!

At the Preston convention that I have mentioned before, one year they received a handkerchief from America for a mentally retarded boy. He was about thirteen with the mental age of four or five. This was the first year Wigglesworth had not been at the convention. He had been called home to the presence of God. So a group of us stood around and prayed, asking God to send

His healing power as this handkerchief was laid on the boy as a token of His power.

I did not hear anything for several years but, about five or six years later, a lady came up to me when I was preaching in Preston and said, "Do you remember when we prayed over that handkerchief for the American retarded boy?"

I said, "Yes, I do," and she continued, "I've just had a letter from my friend in America. The boy has just graduated from high school at 18 years of age, having been successful in all his examinations."

His healing had nothing to do with us. It was God Who did it, and He can use one method as well as another.

For example, often Wigglesworth ministered healing without specific prayer, just as Jesus and the disciples sometimes did. (Matt. 10:8, Acts 3:6.) A man from my first pastorate in Coulsdon, Surrey, England, went to hear Wigglesworth when he was preaching nearby. The man was suffering from diabetes and went out for prayer at the end of the afternoon meeting.

Wigglesworth neither prayed for him nor laid hands on him, but simply said, "Go home, you're healed."

The man stayed on for the evening service, and as he had felt nothing when the evangelist spoke to him in the afternoon, he went forward again when the sick were called.

Wigglesworth looked at him severely and said, "I told you to go home. You are healed." The young man did go home, and he was healed.

A lady in New York went to him suffering from an ingrown toenail, and he simply said, "In the name of Jesus, stamp your foot!" It took courage because of the pain she felt, but she did it, and the toe was healed.

Another lady, from Raleigh, Essex, England, went for prayer for an ulcerated leg. Wigglesworth said, "Be healed!" Then he said, "Now, run!" She burst out laughing, because she had known his methods and had made up her mind not to do anything spectacular.

He repeated, "I said, 'Run, woman, run!'"

And, laughing all the way, she ran and was instantly healed. I was there at the time and enjoyed the whole scene.

Chapter 16:

"Wholesale" and "Retail" Healings

*D*uring Wigglesworth's first series of meetings in Sweden in 1920, he was permitted to hold a service on the strict condition that he did not lay hands on the sick. The authorities thought that would create crowd scenes they did not have enough police available to handle.

When he saw the needs of the people present in the open-air meeting, he was deeply moved and sought God's direction on what to do, since he was not allowed to lay hands on them. The Lord made clear to him that he was to get all the sick people to stand to their feet where they were.

Then he said, "I'm not going to touch any of you."

At the Lord's direction, he turned his attention to a lady standing on a rock and told her to place her hands on her body where the sickness was. She did, and he prayed. She cried out, "I'm healed." He then had all the others lay hands on themselves, and he prayed for their healings.

God showed Wigglesworth that it was His power and not any particular method that brought healing. He playfully called this "wholesale healing." Praying individually for people was "retail healing." If the crowds seeking healing were very large, he would use the first method after that. But if it was possible, he would use the second.

Add Patience to Faith

One day, while I was preaching at Preston, and Wigglesworth was my chairman, I really got the people's attention by starting my message out this way:

"Brother Wigglesworth is wrong, you know. He says, 'Only believe,' but that's not all." By this time, I had his attention as well as their's!

I continued, "In Hebrews 6:12, it says we are to be followers of them who through faith *and* patience inherit the promises. We need to add patience to faith."

Wigglesworth relaxed and called out, "You're right, brother, you're right. Preach it!"

A young lady living at Southsea, on the English south coast, was paralyzed from the waist down. A devoted Christian, she came across James 5:14-16 about the elders of the church anointing the sick with oil. When her pastor visited her, she showed it to him and asked him to anoint her with oil and pray for her. But he did not believe that promise was for today and declined.

Later, the assistant pastor visited her, and she asked him. Without hesitation, he agreed. Her mother found a bottle of oil, and the young minister anointed the girl and prayed for her.

Nothing happened, but the girl told everyone who visited her, "Look what I have found in the Bible, and I've had this done to me."

There was no immediate change. Weeks passed into months, and after six months, she suddenly experienced great pain. Her legs crossed, and she was in worse condition than before.

However, she said often through her tears, "Look what I've found in the Bible, and I've had this done to me."

Another three months went by. One night, in extreme pain, she asked her mother not to touch her to prepare her for sleep. Her mother left the room weeping. The girl lay quietly praying. Suddenly the room was alight with the presence of Jesus, and she heard His voice, "Arise in this thy strength."

Her legs instantly uncrossed. Miraculously, her muscles were strengthened. She rose from bed, went to the door of her room, and called, "Mummy, Mummy, come and see what Jesus has done for me." Her mother fainted!

That young lady later became a member of the church of Pastor F. R. Barnes, for many years a member of the executive council of the Assemblies of God of Great Britain and Ireland. He himself recounted this incident to me, assuring me of its authenticity. Through faith and patience, that young lady inherited the promise.

Whatever the situation, Wigglesworth focused on Christ. He had unquestionable confidence in Him. He saw sickness and oppression as the works of the devil (1 John 3:8), and in Christ's name, moved against Satan with holy violence. He even faced and overcame death in some instances.

However, there were other instances when he had no freedom to pray for certain people. One of the deacons of our church brought a sick neighbor. God's servant just took one look at him and said, "You ought to be in your coffin." He challenged the man to be ready, and a timely challenge it was — within two weeks the man was dead.

Usually it was not so dramatic as that. On one occasion he was asked to pray for a wealthy lady. He discerned pride and materialism in her and said, "You're not ready for me yet."

She was angry at first, but later broke down before the Lord. Wigglesworth prayed for her, and she was healed.

One day, I introduced him to a young minister. After the man left us, Wigglesworth asked me, "What's wrong with that man?"

I told him the man's wife had died six months earlier, and he began to weep, saying no man who has not been through such a loss can begin to understand what it means. He then told me that when his wife died, he had called her back from the dead, but God spoke to him: "Leave her, Smith, she is mine." He said it was the greatest and costliest test of obedience.

To John Carter, Smith Wigglesworth said:

"We need to wake up and be on stretch to believe God. Before God could bring me to this place, He has broken me a thousand times. I have wept. I have travailed many a night till God broke me. It seems that until God has mowed you down, you never can have this longsuffering for others."

The Final Call

Wigglesworth's homecall was as unusual as his life. In 1947, at almost eighty-eight years of age, he was attending the funeral of his dear friend, Pastor Wilfred Richardson, and entered Glad Tidings Hall in Wakefield, Yorkshire, praising the Lord.

He was taken to the vestry, the small room used for the ministers, where he greeted several colleagues and inquired after the health of the daughter of one of them. The news was not good. Wigglesworth sighed, stumbled, and his spirit departed.

His grandson, Leslie, said, "He sighed, and he died."

His earthly life was over. But, now, more than forty years later, his ministry is touching more lives than ever. If it has been true of any human being, it is true of Wigglesworth: "He being dead yet speaketh" (Heb. 11:4).

Conclusion:

Glimpses of the Future

*W*hen in New Zealand in 1922, a young preacher remarked to Wigglesworth, "One is tempted to envy you for the great success you have had."

He replied, "Young man, it is the other way around. I feel like envying you. I have had three visions — three only. The first two already have come to pass, but the third is yet to be fulfilled. I will most likely pass on to my reward, but you are a young man, and you most likely will be in what I saw."

He paused, then burst out, "Oh, it was amazing! Amazing!"

"What was amazing?" the young man asked.

"Oh," said Wigglesworth, "I cannot tell God's secrets, but you will remember what I saw — this revival we have had (the Pentecostal revival) is nothing to what God is yet going to do."

In recounting this, the young preacher went on to say, "This was clearly prophetic and spoken with much power. It was evident that the evangelist had a special vision granted to him of the coming outpouring of the Spirit in an unprecedented effusion in the days just before our Lord comes to snatch away the Church."[1]

---

[1] *New Zealand's Greatest Revival*, p. 29.

The story often has been told of Wigglesworth's prophecy over the late David du Plessis. He was conducting a crusade in David's church in South Africa. Early one morning, he walked into David's office and, without greeting, declared to him that in the last days, before Jesus returned, there would be a move of the Holy Spirit surpassing all previous moves. It would overrun all boundaries, national and denominational. David du Plessis, he declared, would be a principal instrument in God's hand to bring this to pass.

In 1942, Wigglesworth talked to me about this prophecy, saying that he would not live to see this glorious revival. He died in 1947, the year that David du Plessis arrived from South Africa at the World Pentecostal Conference in Zurich, Switzerland. From that point, his ministry and influence spread.

Du Plessis carried the full message of Pentecost into areas no one thought it would ever go and prepared the way for the Charismatic Renewal, which developed in an astonishing way during the 1960s and 1970s. He became known as "Mr. Pentecost," and met with heads of otherwise liberal denominations and with the Pope in Rome.

A week before his death, Wigglesworth prophesied again during a week-long crusade. This time, he foretold a second move of the Spirit. The first move would bring the restoration of the gifts of the Spirit; the second would bring a revival of emphasis on the Word of God.

He said, "When these two moves of the Spirit combine, we shall see the greatest move the Church of Jesus Christ has ever seen."

Already there are signs that this is beginning to develop.

Tribute to
Smith Wigglesworth

He Was Not . . . God Took Him
The Home Call of Smith Wigglesworth
by James Salter

---

*The following tribute was written immediately after the death of
Smith Wigglesworth, by his son-in-law, James Salter. Wigglesworth
called his daughter and her husband, "our Alice" and "my son,
Salter." He lived with them, and they were intimately acquainted
with his life and ministry for very many years. This tribute first
was published on March 28, 1947, two weeks after the homecall
of Brother Wigglesworth, in* Redemption Tidings, *official
magazine of the Assemblies of God of Great Britain and Ireland
and is used by kind permission of the editor.*

On March 12, in the vestry of Glad Tidings Hall,
Wakefield, Mr. Smith Wigglesworth discarded his earthly
house of this tabernacle. He had gone there to attend the
funeral service of Mr. Wilfred Richardson, a lifelong
friend, and while waiting for the meeting to commence,
he suddenly collapsed, and without any pain or recovering
consciousness, he went to be with Christ, dying the death
of the righteous.

He would have attained his 88th birthday on June 10th
and had had a saving knowledge of the Lord Jesus for

nearly eighty years. Although so young at the time, his spiritual awakening must have been very impressive for, as he so often told us, he knelt to kiss the daisies growing in the field and sang with the birds in the lanes of his native village.

Beginning to work in a mill about that time, his childish trust sustained him in his daylight-to-dark employment. He used to take pride in pointing to the mill where he worked and telling us how he was often very tired and how to his boyish question, "How much longer?" his father would reply, "Night always comes to those who work, my lad!"

He grew in grace and zeal for God, and his highest happiness was found in pointing others to the Lord Jesus, and he tramped the country roads with that one purpose.

"Have you been talking to a man about his soul?" his mother asked him one day.

"Mother, you know I am always doing that," he replied. "But why do you ask?"

"Because," she answered, "Mr. So-and-So has had an accident and is dying, and he wishes me to tell you he decided for Christ the last time you spoke to him."

To his dying day, he lived for this one thing, rarely coming home morning, afternoon, or night but what he had led someone to the Lord or ministered healing to a needy person.

When he commenced his healing ministry, he was officially and publicly derided by many of his old friends, but as the years went by, he was able to heap coals of fire on their heads by ministering to their needy bodies. Many who had scorned and scoffed publicly, later sought him privately and at nighttime for the blessing of the effectual and fervent prayers of the righteous man.

Lacking the advantage of a normal early education, he never read books. This shut him off from many things and left him not conversant with general topics. After the death of his wife, thirty-four years before, he was naturally a lonely man. These things drove him to God and His Word, and he never considered himself fully dressed unless he had a copy of the Scriptures in his pocket. In that way, he came to know God to a degree attained by very few folks.

He was intimate with God before 1914, but in that year, God sent him to America for the first time, as he used to say, "to teach me geography." Having recently lost his wife, the one who had done much to make him thus far, he went abroad in an abandonment to God that found a continent-wide fruition in all the United States and Mexico. From that time, his gifts made room for him, and continents and countries opened wide to the plumber-preacher.

New Zealand was swept, Colombo in Ceylon shaken, Sweden roused, Switzerland stormed, Norway inflamed, and California stirred to its depth, as God confirmed His Word through this "mantled man." The permanence of these works is visible to this day in that souls were saved, bodies were healed, lives changed and delivered, and assemblies of believers were established.

Every mail brings testimonies from those who have read his book, *Ever-Increasing Faith*, telling of blessings to soul and body received through its ministry. Every kind of disease has succumbed to the healing power of God, as readers have found and exercised faith in the Living God, and in every country, its simple and sufficient message "only believe" has linked tens of thousands of people to the living, saving, healing, victorious Lord Jesus.

His preaching was purely inspirational, and at times his words and their meanings were not easy to follow, but that "indefinable something which makes all the difference" rarely was lacking from his ministry, and under it, his hearers took spiritual strides and made godly progress.

He was the modern "apostle of faith," but his faith was not the dormant kind. One of his slogans was "Faith is an act," and said he, "the acts of the apostles is called the Acts of the Apostles because the apostles acted.

He probably was much misunderstood in his ministry to the sick, and he suffered considerably because of personal remarks, and so forth, although he triumphed in his spirit over such things. As one who shared his work over many years and in many countries, I am convinced he enjoyed a holy insight at such times, and he saw and heard things unspeakable, as frequently "two pierced hands" shared with him the "laying on of hands" in the destroying of the works of the devil.

His creed was not a big one, but it was the "most surely believed" type. He was valiant for the truth and absolutely uncompromising even in the matter of details. The Fellowship of Pentecostal folk owes much to him for his unswerving adherence to the peculiar aspect of their testimony.

His body, waiting interment, lies a few feet from me as I write, and piled high in front of me are letters, telegrams, and cables. "$300 ready to bring you by plane to . . . ," reads one. Another, arriving only a few hours after he died, reads: "Planes are very comfortable these days. We want you in New York for our fortieth anniversary meetings in May. Be sure to come."

Some others received since his death say of him:

"A beautiful and lovely character; one of God's sweet men."

"That humble, yet great, master of victorious faith."

"A great loss to the whole church which owes much to his inspiring ministry and steadfast example in the things which we stand for."

"He has winged his way to be with Christ in a sudden and triumphant translation."

"May his mantle of faith, zeal, and power fall upon the generations following to glorify their fathers' God."

"Triumphant faith; whose faith follow."

"It behooves us all to take up the torch which he has laid aside and burn and blaze for God."

"Smith Wigglesworth walked with God, and he was not, for God took him."

In concluding, is it too much to hope that what he has sown during the past sixty years may bear an abundant harvest and result in a world-changing revival of soul-saving, Spirit-filling, body-healing, and delivering which will usher in the return of the Lord Jesus and the rapture of His waiting people?

Appendix:

New Zealand Sermons

{The following messages were preached by Smith Wigglesworth in Wellington, New Zealand, in May 1922. They were transcribed by the Rev. Harry V. Roberts, and are published by the kind permission of his grandson, the Rev. Ian Bilby, president of the Elim Church of New Zealand.}

Sanctification of the Spirit

I want to read to you a few verses from First Peter 1. I believe that God wants to speak to us to strengthen our position in faith and grace.

Beloved, I want you to understand that you will get more than you came for. There is not a person who hears me will get what he came for. God gives you more. No man gets his answers to his prayers. He never does, for God answer his prayers abundantly above what he asks or thinks.

Don't say, "I got nothing."

You'll get as much as you came for and more. But if your minds are not willing to be yielded, and your heart not sufficiently consecrated, you will find that you are limited on that line, because the heart is the place of reception. God wants you to have receptive hearts to take in the mind of God. These wonderful Scriptures are full of life-giving power. Let us read the first and second verses. There are some words there I ought to lay emphasis on.

> Peter, an apostle of Jesus Christ, to the strangers scattered throughout Pontus, Galatia, Cappadocia, Asia and Bithynia,
>
> Elect according to the foreknowledge of God the Father, through sanctification of the Spirit, unto obedience and sprinkling of the blood of Jesus Christ: grace to you, and peace be multiplied.
>
> 1 Peter 1:1,2

I want you to notice that in all times, in all histories of the world, whenever there has been a divine rising or revelation — God coming forth with new dispensational orders of the Spirit — you will find that there have been persecutions. You take the case of the three Hebrew young men, or Daniel, or Jeremiah. With any person in the old dispensation, as much as in the new, when the Spirit of the Lord has been moving mightily, there has arisen trouble and difficulty. What for? Because of three things very much against revelations of God and the Spirit of God.

First, humanity — flesh — natural things are against divine things. Evil powers work upon this position of the human life, and especially when the will is unyielded to God, then the powers of darkness arise up against the powers of divine order, but they never defeat them. Divine order is very often in a minority, yet always in majority. Did I say that right? Yes, and I meant it also. You have no need to fear, truth stands eternal. Wickedness may increase and abound, but when the Lord raises His flag over the saint, it is victory; though it is in minority it always triumphs.

I want you to notice the first verse because it says *scattered*, meaning to say they did not get much of the liberty of meeting together. They were driven from place to place. Even in the days of John Knox, the people who served God had to be in close quarters, because they were persecuted, hauled before judges, and destroyed in all sorts of ways. They were in minority but swept through in victory. So may God bring us into perfect order that we may understand these days that we may be in Wellington in minority, yet in majority.

The Holy Ghost wants us to understand our privileges, elect, according to the foreknowledge of God through sanctification of the Spirit. Now this word "sanctification of the Spirit" is not on the lines of sin cleansing. It is a higher order than redemption work. The blood of Jesus is rich unto all, powerful and cleansing. It takes away other powers and transforms us by the power of God. But when sin is gone, yes, when we are clean and know we have the Word of God right in us, and the power of the Spirit is bringing us to a place where we triumph, then comes revelation by the power of the Spirit lifting us to higher ground, into the fullness of God, unveiling Christ in such a way. It is called sanctification of the Spirit.

"Sanctification of the Spirit," elect, according to the foreknowledge of God. I don't want you to stumble at the word *elect*, it is a blessed word. You might say you are all elect; everyone in this place could say you are elected. God has designed that all men should be saved — this is election. Whether you accept, and come into your election, whether you prove yourself worthy of your election, whether you have done this, I don't know. But this is your election, your sanctification, to be seated at the right hand of God.

The word *election* is a very precious word. To be foreordained, predestinated — these are words that God has designed before the world was to bring us into triumph and victory in Christ. Some people play around and make it a goal. They say, "Oh, well, you see, we are elected. We are all right."

They say they are elected to be saved, and I believe these people are very diplomatic (because) they believe others can be elected to be damned. It is not true! Everybody is elected to be saved, but whether they come into it or not is another thing.

Many don't come into salvation because the god of this world has blinded their eyes lest the light of the glorious gospel should shine unto them. What does it mean? It means this, that Satan has got mastery over their minds, and they have an ear to listen to corruptible things.

Beloved, I want you to see this election I am speaking about, to catch a glimpse of heaven, with our heart always on the wing, where you grasp everything spiritual, when everything divine makes you hungry, everything seasonable in spiritual fidelity will make you long after it.

If I came here in a year's time I should see this kind of election going right forward, always full, never having a bad report, where you see Christ, and every day growing in the knowledge of God.

It is through sanctification of the Spirit unto obedience and sprinkling of the blood of Jesus Christ. There is no sanctification, if it is not sanctification unto obedience. There would be no trouble with any of us if we would come definitely to a place where we understood the Word that Jesus said: "For their sakes I sanctify myself, that they also might be sanctified through the truth." (John 17:19).

No child of God ever questions the Word of God. What do I mean? The Word of God is clear on breaking of bread, the Word of God is clear on water baptism, and things like that.

No person who is going on to the obedience and sanctification of the spirit by election will pray over that Word. The Word is to be swallowed, not prayed over!

If you ever pray over the Word of God there is some disobedience; *there is some disobedience;* you are not willing to obey. If you come into obedience on the Word of God, and it says anything about water baptism, you will obey; if it says anything about speaking in tongues, you will obey; if it says anything about breaking of bread and assembling of yourselves together, you will obey. If you come into the election of the sanctification of the Spirit, you will be obedient in everything concerning that Word. In the measure you are not obedient, you have not come into the sanctification of the Spirit.

A little thing spoils many good things. You hear people say, "He's very good, but . . . ," "Mrs. X is excellent, but . . . ." There are no buts in the sanctification of the Spirit. *But* and *if* are gone, and it is "I shall," "I will," all the way through.

Beloved, don't have any buts, for if you do there is something not yielded to the Spirit. I do pray God the Holy Ghost that we may be willing to yield ourselves to the sanctification of the Spirit, that we may be in the mind of God in the election, that we may have the mind of God in the possession of it.

Perhaps to encourage you people it would be helpful to prove to you what election is. I am speaking to believers. If you had to search your heart (as to) why you have been attending these meetings, you would not say "because of Wigglesworth." It would be a mistake. But if you felt in you a holy calling, or strange inward longing for more of God, you could say it was sanctification of the Spirit that was drawing you. Only He who elected you could do that!

There are people of all ages here in this place, and if I were to say to you, "Stand up all who never remembered the time when the Spirit did not strive with you," it would be marvellous how many would stand. What do you call it? It is God moving upon you, bringing you in.

When I think of my own case, on my mother's side and on my father's side there was no desire for God. Yet in my earliest infancy I was strangely moved upon by the Spirit. At eight years, I was definitely saved. At nine years the Spirit came upon me (and it was) just the same when I spoke with tongues — elect according to the foreknowledge of God. There are people in this place who have the same experience.

It is a most blessed thought that we have a God of love, compassion, and grace who wills not the death of one sinner. God makes it possible for all men to be saved. He gave Jesus, His well-beloved Son, to die for the sins of the people. It is true He took our sins. It is true He paid the price for the whole world. It is true He gave Himself a ransom for many. It is true, beloved! For whom? For "whosoever will."

What about the others? It would have to be a direct refusal of the blood of Jesus, a refusal to have Christ reign over them. Whosoever will, and whosoever won't! And there are people that won't. I say again the god of this world has blinded their minds lest the light of the Gospel shine unto them.

Through sanctification of the Spirit, you will find out that you get to a place where you are not disturbed. There is a peace in sanctification of the Spirit, because it has a place of revelation, taking you into heavenly places. It has a place where God speaks and makes Himself known to you. When you are face to face with God, you qet a peace which passes all understanding, lifting you from state to state of inexpressible wonderment. It is really wonderful!

O, this is like heaven to me,
Yes, this is like heaven to me;
I've crossed over Jordan to Canaan's fair land,
And this is like heaven to me.

Now look at verse three:

> Blessed be the God and Father of our Lord Jesus Christ, which
> according to his abundant mercy hath begotten us again unto
> a lively hope by the resurrection of Jesus Christ from the dead.
>
> 1 Peter 1:3

Lively hope! We cannot pass that, because this sanctification of the Spirit brought us into this definite line with this wonderful position of the glory of God. I want to keep before us the glory of it, the joy of it, a "lively hope." Now a lively hope is exactly opposite to dead!

Lively hope is movement.

Lively hope is looking into.

Lively hope is pressing into.

Lively hope is leaving everything behind you.

Lively hope is keeping the vision.

Lively hope sees Him coming!

Lively hope, you live in! You are not trying to make yourself feel that you are believing. The lively hope is ready, waiting, filled with the joy of expectation of the King. Praise the Lord!

I want you to know that God has this in mind for you. If you possess it, you will love others towards God. They will see the real joy of expectation that will come forth with manifestation, then realization. Pray God, the Holy Ghost, that He will move you that way.

Come now, beloved, I want to raise your hopes into such activity, into such joyful experience, that when you go away from this meeting you will have such joy that you will only walk if you cannot run!

Now I trust that you will be so reconciled to God that there is not one thing that would interfere with you having this lively hope. If you have any love for the world you cannot have it, because Jesus is not coming for the world. He is coming to the heavenlies, and all the heavenlies are going to Him. There is nothing but joy there! The pride of life is contrary to the lively hope, because of the greatness of the multi-magnitudinous glories of eternity, which are placed before Him with exceeding joy.

[Interpretation of Tongues: "The joy of the Lord is everything. The soul lifteth up like the golden grain ready to be ingathered for the great sheaf. All are ready, waiting, rejoicing, longing for Him, till they cry, 'Lord Jesus, we cannot wait longer.' "]

What a wonderful expression of the Holy Ghost to the soul is in interpretation! How He loves us, hovers over us, rejoices in us. Our cup is full and running over. The joy of the Lord is your strength. You have a right to be in these glorious places. It is the purpose of God for your soul.

> To an inheritance incorruptible, and undefiled, and that fadeth not away, reserved in heaven for you.

> 1 Peter 1:4

First, incorruptible. Second, undefiled. Third, fadeth not away. Fourth, reserved in heaven for you. Glory to God! I tell you it is great, very great. May the Lord help you to thirst after this glorious life of Jesus. Oh, brother, it is more than new wine. The

Holy Ghost is the manifestation of the glories of the new creation. *An inheritance incorruptible.*

Incorruptible is one of those delightful words God wants all the saints to grasp — everything corruptible, everything seen, fades away.

Incorruptible is that which eternal, everlasting, divine, and therefore spiritual. It brings us to a place where God is really in the midst. This is one part of our inheritance in the Spirit, one part only. Oh, how beautiful, perfected for ever! No spot, no wrinkle, holy, absolutely pure, all traces of sin withered.

Beloved, God means it for us this morning. Every soul in this place must reach out to this ideal. God has ten thousand more thoughts for you than you have for yourself. The grace of God is going to move us on to an inheritance incorruptible, that fadeth not away.

Fadeth not away! What a heaven of bliss, what a joy of delight, what a foretaste of heaven on earth. Cheerfully go to the work you have to do, because of tomorrow (when you) will be in the presence of the King, with the Lord for ever, an inheritance that fadeth not away.

Perfect Rest

I would like you to read Second Corinthians 10:4,5:

> For the weapons of our warfare are not carnal, but mighty through God to the pulling down of strong holds;
>
> Casting down imaginations, and every high thing that exalteth itself against the knowledge of God, and bringing into captivity every thought to the obedience of Christ.

Now the Holy Ghost will take the Word, making it powerful in you till every evil thing that presents itself against the obedience and fullness of Christ would absolutely wither away. I want to show you this morning the need of the baptism of the Holy Ghost, by which you know there is perfect rest when you are filled with the Holy Ghost. I want you to see perfect rest in this place.

I want you to see Jesus. He was filled with the Holy Ghost. The storm began so terribly. The ship filled with water. He lay asleep. Perfect rest. When the disciples cried, "Master, we perish," Jesus rose, filled with the Holy Ghost, and rebuked the wind and spoke His peace.

Come a little nearer. I want you to see that this Holy Ghost, this divine Person, has to get so deep into us that He has to destroy every evil thing. Quick, powerful, sharper than any two-edged sword, piercing even to the dividing asunder of soul and spirit, and of the joints and marrow. (Heb. 4:12.)

Some people get pain in their life after being saved because of soulishness. Any amount of saved people are soulish. They're in Romans 7. They want to do good but find evil. They continue to do the thing they hate to do. What is up?

They need the baptism of the Holy Ghost, for then the Holy Ghost will so reveal the Word that it will be like a sword. It will cut between the soul and the spirit, till a man can no more long for indulgence in things contrary to the mind of God and the will of God. Don't you want rest? How long are you going to be before you enter into that rest? God wants you to enter that rest.

> For he that is entered into his rest, he also hath ceased from his own works, as God did from his.
> Let us labour therefore to enter into that rest, lest any man fall after the same example of unbelief.
>
> Hebrews 4:10,11

Enter into rest, get filled with the Holy Ghost, and unbelief will depart. When they entered in they were safe from unbelief, and unbelief is sin. It is the greatest sin because it hinders you from all blessings.

There is another word that would be helpful this morning, and I want you to take notice of it because it is important. It is verse 12 of Hebrews 4:

> For the word of God is quick, and powerful, and sharper than any two-edged sword, piercing even to the dividing asunder of soul and spirit, and of the joints and marrow, and is a discerner of the thoughts and intents of the heart.

How we need the Holy Ghost! Now probably when You go outside you will say, "He preached more about the Holy Ghost than anything."

It is not so. My heart is so full of this truth that Jesus is the Word. It takes the Holy Ghost to make the Word active. Jesus is the Word that is mighty by the power of the Spirit to the pulling down of strongholds, moving upon us so that the power of God is seen upon us.

[Interpretation of Tongues: "God hath designed the fullness of the Gospel in its perfection and entirety that where the breath of heaven breathes upon it, the Gospel which is the power of God unto salvation makes everything form in perfect union with divine power, till the whole man becomes a lovely hope — filled with life, filled with fidelity."]

Remember that Jesus is all fullness. Remember Jesus was the fullness of the Godhead. The Holy Ghost makes Him so precious that: "It's all right now, it's all right now, For Jesus is my Saviour, and it's all right now."

I want you all to have a share! Oh, for the Holy Ghost to come with freshness upon us, then you all could sing, "It's all right now!" Let me encourage you. God is a God of encouragement. Now turn to Hebrews 4:13:

> Neither is there any creature that is not manifest in his sight: but all things are naked and opened to the eyes of him with whom we have to do.

No creature is hid from His sight, all are naked before Him. When God speaks of nakedness He does not mean that He looks at flesh without clothing. He looks at our spiritual lack, and desires that we are clothed with Christ within. He sees your weakness, your sorrow of heart. He is looking right into you now. Oh, what does He see?

> Seeing then that we have a great high priest, that is passed into the heavens, Jesus the Son of God, let us hold fast our profession.
>
> Hebrews 4:14

What is our profession? I have heard so many people testifying about their profession. Some said, "Thank God He has baptized me with the Holy Ghost." That is my profession, is it yours? That is the profession of the Bible, and God wants to make it your profession. You have a whole Christ, a full redemption. You have to be filled with the Holy Ghost, a channel for Him to flow through. Oh, the glorious liberty of the gospel of God's power!

Heaven has begun with me,
I am happy now, and free
Since the Comforter has come,
Since the Comforter has come.

It's all there. I know that God has designed this fullness, this rest, this perfect rest. He has designed it, and there ought not to be a wrinkle, a spot, a blemish. The Word of God says "blameless." Praise the Lord for such a wonderful, glorious inheritance, through Him that loved us. Hallelujah!

Beloved, you must come in, every one of you. This morning's meeting is to open the door of your heart so that God can move in so that if you were to go away to live in some solitary place, you would be full there the same as in the Wellington Assembly. It would make no difference. The authorities tried to destroy John and sent him to the Isle of Patmos, but on a desert island he was "in the Spirit." It is possible to be in the Spirit wherever you are, in all circumstances.

> For we have not an high priest which cannot be touched with the feeling of our infirmities; but was in all points tempted like as we are, yet without sin.
>
> Hebrews 4:15

There He is! There is the pattern! There is the Lord! You say, "Tell me something wonderful about Him." I will tell you this, He loved us to the end. He had faith in us right to the end.

"There remaineth therefore a rest to the people of God" (Heb. 4:9). Some say, "O, yes, it is a rest up there." No! No! No! *This* rest is here, where we cease from our own works, this day!

I came to this meeting this morning entirely shut in with God, and if ever God spoke in a meeting He has spoken this morning.

I may have been straight and plain on some lines, but I had such a vision of Wellington. I saw clearly people were resisting the Holy Ghost, as much as when Stephen said, "Ye stiffnecked and uncircumcised in heart and ears, ye do always resist the Holy Ghost: as your fathers did, so do ye" (Acts 7:51).

Oh, if you won't resist the Holy Ghost the power of God will melt you down. The Holy Ghost will so take charge of you that you will be filled to the uttermost with the overflowing of His grace.

The Gifts of the Spirit:
Prophecy and Tongues

It is necessary that we have a great desire for spiritual gifts. God must bring us into a place where we thirst after them. They are necessary. They are important. May we by the grace of God see their importance, so that we may be used for God's glory.

First, *Prophecy*. If you are saved here this morning, it is because of some person (who) was inspired and loved upon by the Spirit of Jesus to let the light of this glorious gospel come to you. Sometimes I think we miss what God has for us in the Gospels. I want you to see a word God has for us. It is pure gospel truth.

> Who hath saved us, and called us with a holy calling, not according to our works, but according to his own purpose and grace, which was given us in Christ Jesus before the world began,
>
> But is now made manifest by the appearing of Jesus Christ, who hath abolished death, and hath brought life and immortality to light through the gospel.
>
> 2 Timothy 1:9,10

The Lord help us to see that above all, whatever we do, we seek the gift of prophecy. Now there are three classes of prophecy I want to speak about.

Bubbling Up: There is a prophetic utterance which you will find very often when I am speaking. So often when I am speaking the Holy Ghost speaks through me in a flow of language. This is prophetic utterance which every Spirit-baptized believer ought to have. Holy Ghost ministry, Holy Ghost language, and Holy Ghost thought. Standing there clothed upon with prophetic utterances, always coinciding with God's will.

Another kind of prophecy is *testimony*. If you people in this Town Hall will come to meetings filled with the Holy Ghost, and there is a chance to qive your testimony, let it be a Holy Ghost utterance. Then people will feel that it is the Holy Ghost. It will be different from any human testimony. In yourself, you can give your testimony until it is barren! "For the testimony of Jesus is the spirit of prophecy" (Rev. 19:10). Jesus said His words are spirit and life.

The last kind of prophecy is *the prophetic utterance in the assembly,* when every one knows it is from the Lord.

> But he that prophesieth speaketh unto men to edification, and exhortation, and comfort.
>
> 1 Corinthians 14:3

Prophecy will not be denunciation. God wants you to have this prophecy, so that you rise up as if you had risen up out of death into life. You would be uttering divine revelation and consolation. It might be on the line of the coming of the Lord, or the atoning blood, or about the moving of the Spirit in our midst; but it will be to comfort, console and edify.

> For he that speaketh in an unknown tongue speaketh not unto men, but unto God: for no man understandeth him; howbeit in the spirit he speaketh mysteries.
>
> 1 Corinthians 14:2

This is a wonderful verse for anyone who has had a weary day, or is going through hard trials. You get before the Lord with such an utterance, and you will find that God by His Spirit will lift you, move you. It has not to be interpreted, it is spoken to God by the Spirit.

Laughter in the Holy Ghost: It may seem to some people very strange, but I have seen people come into a meeting down and out, exhausted. The power of God has come on them with lauqhter. Laughter in the Holy Ghost brings you out of everything! It is a thing you cannot create. The Holy Ghost laughs through you. You laugh from the inside. The whole body is so full of the Spirit of life from above that you are altogether new. For God to come into a needy soul and create laughter within is very wonderful.

Praying in the Spirit: Now we come to another wonderful word which is important. We must understand this morning that we are at the footstool of grace, and God the Holy Ghost is our Teacher. We must listen to see what God has to say to us at this time.

Some people think there is only one kind of prayer that brings down blessing, but you will find when God the Holy Ghost takes you, He can through one pure heart bring revival in spite of every power in the world. This verse we have been looking at is an unknown Scripture except to those who have received the Holy Ghost. Who is speaking? The Holy Spirit. To whom? To God. Where shall we find a verse to give us clear revelation on this? In Romans 8:26,27:

> Likewise the Spirit also helpeth our infirmities: for we know not what we should pray for as we ought: but the Spirit itself maketh intercession for us with groanings that cannot be uttered.

> And he that searcheth the hearts knoweth what is the mind of the Spirit, because he maketh intercession for the saints according to the will of God.

It is not you, remember! It is the Spirit that is in you, that is, the Holy Ghost.

Jesus is the Advocate.

The Father is the Answerer.

The Holy Spirit is the Pray-er.

The Spirit searches the hearts. Right in the heart God is searching by the light of His Spirit. When God is moving in the heart, the Spirit begins to pray that God will be satisfied. The Holy Spirit prays through you, and brings down the blessing!

[Tongues with interpretation: "The Lord Himself, it is He which hath opened into our heart His great fullness and now through the power of Himself is bringing out the great cry of the soul, mingled with the Spirit's cry, till heaven bends down and grants."]

I believe it would be helpful for me to tell you about Willie Burton, a missionary leader in Central Africa. He is a man with a big heart, doing a great work for God, a mighty man of God. He took fever and went down into death.

The people said, "He has preached his last. What shall we do?"

All their hopes were blighted. They stood there brokenhearted. They left him for dead. In a moment, without any signal, he stood in the midst of them. They could not understand it. He told them that he came to himself feeling a warmth through his body, right through. He rose, perfectly healed. It was a mystery, until he came to London. (There) he told the people (in a meeting) how he had been left for dead, and how he was raised up.

A lady came to him afterwards and asked, "Do you keep a diary?"

When he said he did, she told him this:

"One day I went to pray, and as soon as I knelt down you came to my mind. The Spirit of the Lord took hold of me and prayed through me in an unknown tongue. A vision came and I saw you laid out helpless. I cried out in the tongue till I saw you risen up, and go out of that room."

He turned to his diary and found it was exactly the date he had been raised up.

I want you to see that being filled with the Holy Ghost gives you great capabilities, even in your own room! Or anywhere! The Holy Ghost can give you liberty. He is wisdom; He is the spirit of prophecy; He is the Spirit of revelation. Remember God wants you to be filled with the Holy Ghost. Everything about you will be changed by the dynamite of heaven!

There is one very important thing to be dealt with this morning. I want you to see in the first place that he who speaks in an unknown tongue edifies himself. We must be edified before we can edify the church. The Holy Ghost has full charge of wisdom, so He comes to us on wisdom lines. Now in what revelation, or capability, or capacity will the Holy Ghost edify us if we are ready?

Language? None! Inability — full of it! I am here before you this morning as one of the biggest conundrums in the world. All the things about my life are entirely against the likelihood of me standing on this platform before you. There never was a weaker man on a platform. All things about my life are exactly opposite to the likelihood of me standing here, but the Holy Ghost came and brought edification.

I had been reading this Word all my life as well as I could. Then the Holy Ghost came and took hold of it. The Holy Ghost is the breath of it and quickened it to me to edify me, so that

I might edify the church. He gave me language that I cannot speak fast enough. It is there because God has given it.

When the Comforter has come, He teaches you all things. First John 2:20,27 says:

> But ye have an unction from the Holy One, and ye know all things.
>
> But the anointing which ye have received of him abideth in you, and ye need not that any man teach you: but as the same anointing teacheth you of all things, and is truth, and is no lie, and even as it hath taught you, ye shall abide in him.

I am not leaving out the people who are not baptized in the Holy Ghost, but am putting you all as one. Because I believe God wants you all baptized. I believe you will go on until you are.

After you are baptized you may say, "I seem so dry. I don't know where I am."

The Word says you have an unction. Thank God, you have an anointing. The Holy Ghost is wisdom, language, and revelation, and He will teach you all things because of the anointing that abides, because of the Holy One that is in you. These are great and definite positions for us. In the Psalms, you often read "Selah." That means "Stop and think." I want you to think this over.

If the Holy Ghost wants to do anything it is to stir up your faith this morning to believe that this word is God's truth. If you allow yourself to rise up in spirit today, you will edify yourself.

"Lord, lift me up and let me stand,
By faith on heaven's table-land;
Where love, and joy, and light abound,
Lord, plant my feet on higher ground."

George Stormont of Duluth, Minnesota, was born in 1909 in Birmingham, England, and knew Smith Wigglesworth personally as a friend and a colleague for many years. Born again in June, 1918, he has served the Lord faithfully as school teacher, Bible college teacher, pastor, and evangelist.

He entered the full-time ministry in 1933. In addition to pastoring five churches in England, he pastored Duluth Gospel Tabernacle in Duluth for five years. He served as superintendent of Elim Pentecostal Churches, England, for a quarter of a century, and for many years, he was a member of the Elim Church Inc.'s executive presbytery.

In addition, he served as national secretary of the British Pentecostal Fellowship and member of the following missionary councils: Elim Missionary Council, The Pentecostal Jewish Mission, Congo (now Zaire) Evangelistic Mission, and Russian and Eastern European Mission.

In 1963, he was invited to pastor Bethshan Tabernacle, Manchester, at the time the largest Assembly of God church in Great Britain. He transferred his membership then to the Assemblies of God, and in 1974, was elected chairman of the Conference of Assemblies of God.

In addition to pioneering new churches, Stormont has conducted evangelistic and teaching crusades all over the world. Since August, 1982, he retired from pastoring to carry out itinerant ministry as the Lord leads.

He has been married to Ruth Kingston since 1938, and they have two children, Andrew and Deryn.

To contact George Stormont
write:

George Stormont
Duluth Gospel Tabernacle
1515 W. Superior St.
Duluth, MN 55806

*Please include your prayer requests
and comments when you write.*

Other **Living Classic Books** from Harrison House

A Diary of Signs and Wonders — Maria Woodworth-Etter

Questions and Answers on Spiritual Gifts — Howard Carter

Healing the Sick — T. L. Osborn

Smith Wigglesworth Remembered — W. Hacking

Smith Wigglesworth: The Secret of His Power
— Albert Hibbert

Cry of the Spirit — Roberts Liardon

John G. Lake: A Man Without Compromise — Wilford Reidt

Additional copies of
Smith Wigglesworth: A Man Who Walked With God
and George Stormont's
Smith Wigglesworth Biography Teaching Tapes
are available from your local bookstore,
or by writing:

Harrison House
P.O. Box 35035
Tulsa, OK 74153